FROM ROOKIE TO RAINMAKER

HOW TO GROW YOUR LAW BUSINESS

JORYN JENKINS

From Rookie to Rainmaker, How to Grow Your Law Business

Published by Open Palm Press

Cover art by 4EDGE, LLC

First Printing: May 2017
Printed in the United States of America

First Edition: May 2017

Dedication

As my daughter begins her career in a highly entrepreneurial profession, I realize again how difficult it was to open my own law practice. She has sensitized me all over again to the intricacies of marketing oneself to one's prospective clients, teammates, partners, mentors, sponsors, and others, and why that is so critical to the self-employed or small firm lawyer. So, I dedicate this book to Alexis. Thank you, Honey, for teaching me so much, even now, after you're all grown up.

Acknowledgments

I've studied a great many manuscripts to discover the secrets of marketing one's law practice. I've included many of those books in my recommended reading list, but there is one book that stands out from the rest. More than any other, it influenced how I've developed my own marketing plan and the marketing strategies I advocate in this book. That book is *Become a Key Person of Influence*, by Daniel Priestly. I owe Daniel a huge debt for teaching me his marketing tactics, tactics that, once refined to apply to a law practice, helped me to achieve the profile I needed to market Open Palm Law and the new approach to divorce that I have only recently undertaken.

I must specifically thank Attorney Lori Skipper, who was invaluable in working with me on many legal matters, and on this book. In the many years since we began collaborating, both at work, and since she left to establish her own business, she has been my right hand.

There are many others with whom I've partnered who have helped me work the kinks out of some of the ideas contained here, as well as the forms I've created, and with whom I've trained or blogged who have shared their insights and understandings. Both my mentors and my protégés alike have been instrumental in helping me collect information and experience so that I might craft the perfect marketing solution for attorneys. Let there be no doubt how grateful I am to them all.

Marketing is no longer about the stuff that you make, but about the stories you tell.

— Seth Godin

If your stories are all about your . . . services, that's not storytelling. It's a brochure. Give yourself permission to make the story bigger.

— Jay Baer

The key is, no matter what story you tell, make your buyer the hero.

— Chris Brogan

TABLE OF CONTENTS

Introduction

You own a law practice. If you've owned it for a long time, you remember when clients used to find you, referred to you by other lawyers, or by previous clients, or by friends. Perhaps you've been around so long that you recall when they would find you in the yellow pages. But they don't seem to do that anymore, at least not in the numbers they used to. Why is that?

Times change. In recent years, they've changed more and more rapidly. Clients don't shop the way they used to, not for books, not for music, not for clothes, and not for lawyers.

You need the marketing tools. I am here to equip you with those tools.

What are the tools in my toolkit? The first is *Pitch*. Why pitch? Because without "pitch," you can't communicate your passion. Pitch leads into everything else. You must have a perfect pitch before you can effectively use any of the other marketing tools in your toolkit. Pitch at least three times a day.

Pitch everywhere. Pitch in the elevator. Pitch at McDonald's. Pitch while you're on the checkout line at Publix, at Sam's Club, at Sears, at Saks Fifth Avenue. Pitch in church or in synagogue. Pitch at your children's school. Pitch at your board meeting. Pitch when you get a call from a reporter. You have a perfect pitch and you must pitch it regularly and often.

Pitch helps you craft your presentations in all venues and pitch helps you construct your publications. So, after *Pitch*, we'll talk about *Publish*. You must publish regularly and often.

Where do you publish? You publish on-line. You publish in on-line magazines (e-zines) and in paper magazines. You publish books, like this one. You blog; you tweet; you post; you comment. You publish every chance you get and you sometimes create those chances, making them happen.

Once you're publishing, the next obvious tool with which to equip yourself is *Present*. As with *Pitch* and *Publish*, you present as often as possible. You seek out opportunities. You present both formally and impromptu. You create PowerPoints for formal presentations. You produce whiteboard videos for your website and for your one-to-one client presentations. You have YouTube videos and you have Slide Shares.

Profile follows *Present*. Once you've got your pitch down, and you're publishing regularly, and presenting often, you'll learn to maximize the value of everything you do exponentially . . . by purposefully raising your profile. Social media is a big deal these days and it will be for the foreseeable future, so grab hold and hang on tight. It's just not that hard!

And, finally, you'll reach out to others and establish those partnerships to multiply your potential. *Partner.* You'll respond to the phone calls and to the offers to connect on LinkedIn. Partnerships include relationships with people in the media, with community movers and shakers, and with first responders.

All of this takes passion . . . . It takes zeal . . . . It takes work.

And here's how . . . .

MARKETING

Introduction to Marketing

Is marketing a dirty word? Are we used car salesman? Most of us, we lawyers, are, even today, not comfortable with the idea of "marketing."

But think of "marketing" as "educating," as "sharing," as informing the public of what you do and why they might need you to do it for them, and you realize that marketing is not a bad thing.

So how do we market our practices? Let's discuss some preliminary issues before we start with the particulars, the five fortes of effective marketing: attaining your clarity (*Pitch)*, establishing your credibility (*Publish)*, achieving your coherence (*Present*), becoming conspicuous (*Profile*), and enabling your connectivity (*Partner*).

Well, perhaps we should start with a task list. Let's outline your next year of marketing effort and summarize what you should be doing, beginning now and ending a year from now. And, as you review this proposed list, note what's easy, what you've already done, what might not be so easy, and what you might want to focus on, to put extra effort into, and how you might accomplish that, whether it's by doing extra reading, by finding a mentor, or by signing up for a seminar. Keep these notes and, when you've finished reading this book, review them and start acting on them.

Marketing Your Practice

What follows is a task list of the most immediate action items with which you should begin your marketing journey. (We will cover all of these in more detail later.)

Pitch

- Rewrite your resume to emphasize your passion, background, education, nature, and/or experience.
- Create an easy-to-read, single-page self-profile, highlighting your goals, your achievements (what gives you credibility), your interests, and your networks. (See a sample self-profile in Appendix 1.)
- Begin working on your firm brochure. (See the example in Appendix 2.)
- Review your contacts; list all referral sources that you already know, and any that occur to you on this first go-round.
- Schedule one-to-ones with your existing referral sources.
- Craft your first quick pitch.
- Start pitching! Pitch people you meet anywhere, among others. (Gauge your audience's reactions.)
- Work on perfecting your quick pitch, based on your audience's reactions.
- Create your own social pitch.
- Start pitching! Pitch your referral sources, among others. (Gauge your audience's reactions.)
- Work on perfecting your social pitch, based on your audience's reactions.
- List all organizations to which you already belong or to which you should apply.
- Apply to those to which you don't yet belong.
- Assess how best to spend your time in those organizations in order to maximize your exposure. Then get those balls in motion.
    - Volunteer for committee work.
    - Arrange to speak.
    - Attend meetings
    - Host meetings.
- Join a referral-networking group.
- Volunteer for *pro bono* work.
- Seek unusual (newsworthy) cases. (These may be *pro bono* cases.) Then

maximize their media value.

- List your newsworthy cases.
    - Ask the client(s) if you can interview them about their experiences.
    - Arrange for willing clients to sign media releases, like the one you'll find in Appendix 3.
    - Send out press releases about noteworthy cases or other news about your practice, like the one you'll find in Appendix 4.
    - Follow up with anyone in the media whom you know regarding same.
- List the people you know who work in the media.
    - Consider radio, TV, newspapers, magazines, and other media. Don't forget podcasts and e-zines.
    - Contact each one you know and schedule a one-to-one meeting to chat about his work and your efforts to market your practice.
    - Arrange to appear on the show as an expert or to be interviewed.
    - Prepare the interview questions for your appearance. I include the answers, as well, so that the newscaster knows what to expect. An example of one of these is in Appendix 5. Of course, this one is for a collaborative divorce practitioner; yours will look quite different, but should be equally detailed.
- Now update your resume to reflect your pitch, your existing and new publications, your media appearances, etc. Repeat this updating regularly.

Publish

- Review publications from all organizations to which you belong or which are pertinent to your work (newsletters, magazines, e-zines, etc.).
- Contact the publications' editorial boards to determine how articles are submitted and what the requirements are for those articles.
- List topics on which you are knowledgeable and design a writing schedule.
- Submit articles.
- Update your website to reflect your pitch and your existing publications.
- Update your brochure to reflect your pitch, if necessary, and your existing publications.
- If you don't have one yet, start your own blog.
    - Write about the remarkable cases you have had, the clients you have counseled, and the lives you have improved. There's an example of this type of blog in Appendix 6.
    - Write about *The Ten Worst Mistakes* you have witnessed people in the shoes of your clients commit. You can see an example of a blog like this repurposed as a chapter in a book at page 21, herein.
    - Write *The Top Ten Tips* for your clients. I include an example of one of these in the Appendix 7.
    - Write about the issues, whether ethical, procedural, or pragmatic, that you have read about, discussed, been confronted by, or considered, or

    that you might have seen in the news or read on your newsfeed.
    - If you had to prepare a memorandum of law on an unusual issue, turn that memo into a blog.
    - Repurpose your articles (see above) into blogs.
- Join or organize a marketing book club or study group. Start reading books on marketing, pitching, publishing, speaking, etc. (See a sample reading list at Appendix 8.)
- Create your book map (an overview outline of the entire book).
- Create your chapter maps.
- Start writing your book. Aim for 35,000 words.
- Review your old blogs and articles to determine whether you can repurpose any of them to fit as chapters in your book.
- Review your noteworthy cases. Pull material from the file that you can repurpose as a chapter.
- Expand any that require additional discussion to fit as chapters into your book. Aim for 3000 (1000-5000) words for each chapter.
- Decide whether to publish conventionally, publish cooperatively, or self-publish.[1]
- Find an editor.
- Design your book cover.
- Prepare the draft foreword for your foreword author to make his job easier.
- Request a foreword. See Appendix 9 for a sample request.
- Prepare draft book testimonials for your clients and peers to make it easier for them to say "yes" when you ask for the endorsements.
- Request book testimonials from clients, colleagues, and celebrities. I've included some sample requests for you to use in Appendix 10.
- Publish your book.
- Update your pitch to include your book in the credibility piece of it.
- Update your resume to include your book in the publications piece of it.

Present

- Learn to use PowerPoint or some similar presentation program.
- Volunteer for a speakers' bureau and make public appearances every chance you get.
- Contact organizations to which you belong, whether social, cultural, political, professional, religious, or otherwise, and present there, as well.
- Prepare a presentation folder for audience members that includes your one-page profile, your brochure, your business card (my folder has the card printed inside it on the flap), examples of your publications, whether you wrote them or they were written about you, etc.
- Update your website and your brochure to reflect publications, if necessary.

[1] Contact Open Palm Press (Joryn@OpenPalmPress.com) for details on the cooperative option.

- Update your pitch.
- Obtain presentation testimonials. See Appendix 11 for a sample request for such testimonials.

Profile

- Create personal and firm profiles on all social media platforms that make sense to you. Consider:
    - Facebook
    - LinkedIn
    - Twitter
    - Instagram
    - YouTube
    - AVVO
    - Google +
    - Pinterest
    - Slide Share
    - Blogger
- Learn to use each platform.
- Blog consistently, at least once per week.
- Blog on topic. Create a schedule for your 52 blogs this year. Stay on schedule.
- Blog on newsworthy topics, for example:
    - In the news
    - Controversy
    - Trends
    - Case studies
    - Predictions
- Post about your articles, blogs, and other publications.
- Post about your presentations.
    - Post before to advertise the availability of seats.
    - Post after to show the success of the program and your availability to present elsewhere.
    - Post your presentation testimonials.
- Respond to or at least *like* other posts.
- Respond to all comments on your own posts, even if it's just to say "thank you for your comment."
- Join networks like *Help a Reporter Out* (HARO) and stay current on and respond to requests that you might be able to answer.
- Update your website and your brochure to reflect presentations, if necessary.

Partner

- List your key contacts.
- Arrange one-to-ones with them.
- Seek out a mentor you admire and ask him or her to lunch.
- Reach down.
    - Mentor others. Offer your protégés opportunities.
    - Chair committees and, when you do, reach out to younger or less-experienced professionals and offer them seats on the committee or related experiences.

  - Offer to blog with them.
  - Offer to edit their publications.
  - Offer to critique their pitches.
- Reach across.
  - Attend advanced trainings and seek out like-minded professionals. Ask them to join you for one-to-ones over lunch or coffee.
- Reach up.
  - To other professionals in your locale whom you admire.
  - To other professionals on-line for their counsel with issues by which you have been confronted.
  - To other professionals who have a great reputation or influence in the local or on-line community and
    - Offer to blog or to co-author an article or a book with them.
    - Offer to conduct trainings, seminars, or workshops with them.
    - Offer to write anthologies with them.
- Offer seminars and trainings to your community.
- Respond to inquiries of any kind and consider the partnership possibilities.
- Update your website, brochure, and on-line profiles to reflect partnerships.
- As always, update your pitch.
- And now, write your partnership pitch.

THE ART OF RUNNING A SUCCESSFUL PRACTICE (BEFORE YOU BEGIN MARKETING I)

Being an exceptional lawyer does not ensure that you will also be a first-rate businessperson. And, while most law schools do not teach soon-to-be attorneys how to run a law firm, this is a skill set that most law school grads will need to develop to be successful. From investing resources wisely to advertising effectively to allocating time to collectible and lucrative ventures, legal professionals should spend time each day ensuring that they are running their businesses as efficiently and effectively as possible. One way to do this is to attend the right seminars and to read the right books. (See, e.g., *From Lawyer to Law Firm, How to Manage a Successful Law Business*, Miller and Jenkins, Open Palm Press, 2017.)

What are the most important elements of such a venture?

INCREASE YOUR RETENTION OF CLIENTS

Obviously, retention of clients is one of the most important elements to a successful law firm. But many potential clients fall through the cracks because of common mistakes of attorneys and their staffs. So what are these common mistakes?

WEBSITES

Many lawyers include links on their websites that drive potential clients off their page and onto other websites where other lawyers advertise or where clients can search other attorneys. Instead of including AVVO or YP review badges that will direct potential clients to other sites, include this information in your biography.

Also avoid including links to court decisions and statutes that lay people won't understand and that will distract them.

Many lawyer websites do not include easily accessible contact information. Sure, there may be a "contact" tab, but people often get sidetracked before locating the "contact" tab. Make it as easy as possible for visitors to your website to find your contact information by adding a pop-up widget to your site. It allows users to contact you from any page without forcing them to navigate around your site. And by popping up every few seconds, it prompts more site visitors to contact you. Olark is a free website add-on that allows visitors to view your site without having to interact with the widget if they opt not to.

E-MAILS

Another common mistake attorneys make occurs when a potential client e-mails your website. Your inclination may be to respond briefly to her question and provide a phone number for her to contact you. However, take a hint. She already found your website, and, thus, your telephone number, but she chose to e-mail you. It seems to be her preferred form of communication. It may be because she can better choose appropriate times to review and respond to your e-mails. Or she may be a better visual communicator. Or she may not want others to hear her conversation with you or see your number on her phone bill.

Whatever the reason, follow her lead. Be open to e-mailing with her. And, once you have determined that it is safe for your office to contact her, have your office call her for follow ups, rather than putting the burden on her to do so. It can be emotionally difficult for a layperson to reach out to an attorney, so make it as easy on her as possible.

Lastly, remember that she has likely e-mailed several attorneys, so a quick, informative and specific (not canned) response is best. Implement a strategy at your firm to ensure that e-mail inquiries are answered immediately and effectively.

PHONE CALLS

Your staff should have a script of how you would like phone calls answered. After verifying that the caller's case is one which your firm might handle, your staff should tell the caller the benefits of coming in for a consult. Then, rather than asking the caller if she would like to schedule a consultation, the staff member should ask *when* the caller would like to come in, "this week or early next week?" (Have you noticed how waiters and waitresses these days don't ask, "How was your meal?" Instead, they ask "Was the meal great?" This is the same thing. Suggest the answer in the question; make it easy for the caller to say "yes.") Don't give the caller an opportunity to turn down the scheduling of the consultation.

Additionally, when scheduling consultations, be sure to ask her preferred method for you to confirm her appointment, and use that method. The confirmation is important because it may give her the little nudge she needs to actually attend an appointment she may be on the fence about. And verifying her preferred form of communication will help to ensure that she actually receives that confirmation.

TEXTS

Many people now are more comfortable texting, yet many attorneys find it unprofessional. While it may not be appropriate for every communication, like longer messages or when a document needs to be forwarded, texting does have its place for the right client. And if this form of communication puts your client most at ease, then it is the appropriate form of communication. In fact, it may be the casual nature of texting that makes a client less stressed than if you were to e-mail her or call her with the same information. Just be sure to take screen shots of the conversation and print them for your file.

DIRECTIONS

Again, remember to keep it simple for the potential client. Make certain that the client can locate your office easily by ensuring that the various mapping services have your correct address and that they will accurately lead her to that address.

Ambiance

Make a good first impression by having a well-furnished (not necessarily expensive) office and presentable, warm staff. Your décor should reflect your personality and practice style. Also, establish an office protocol for greeting guests with which every staff member is familiar. Every client should be made to feel welcome and comfortable.

On-Line Reviews

Remember to manage your on-line reviews. Don't ignore them. They offer a great source of advertisement. Complete your AVVO profile, Google business page, and Facebook business page, including a picture, so that when potential clients research you, they don't just find a blank page. These are currently the three foremost websites on which potential clients will look for reviews, so don't waste time obtaining reviews on sites where potential clients won't look. Instead, when clients want to leave reviews, direct them to these sites.

Moreover, rather than responding to negative reviews, utilize the dispute policies to have any adverse review removed from the website. Finally, set your e-mail settings so that you receive an alert whenever you receive a review so that you can best manage your on-line reputation.

Explore Unique Advertising Methods

Another way to generate new business is to try out distinctive advertising methods. For example, Craigslist offers free advertising, and it is the first place many people go when they are in need of something, even services, so why wouldn't you advertise there? Advertise in the legal "services" section, and always include a banner with a picture. People are more likely to contact an office when they see a picture of a person. It makes your practice more human and approachable. Be sure that the text of your ad is HTML-formatted so that it is visually pleasing. This first impression is important, so your ad should look as professional as possible.

Check with your state bar association to be sure that your ad is appropriate. Re-post the ad every couple of days, and include optimum search terms so it shows up first on search lists. Vary the times and days when you post it until you determine which dates and times are most effective.

When potential clients contact your firm, ask how they heard of you so that you can track the success of your advertisement methods.

Get Creative with Your Fees and Services

Consider offering upfront flat fees and unbundled services. Divide cases into segments, and have clients retain you a segment at a time for a flat fee that is paid before the representation begins. (Or allow clients to write post-dated checks. Start new matters for $500 down if a client is willing to write bi-weekly, post-dated $500 checks for the remainder of the flat fee.) Once that segment is completed, if the client wishes, he can re-retain you to continue with the case for an additional flat fee. Make sure that the client understands when each segment ends and when a new flat fee and re-retention will be required.

By offering flat fees, you remove the tension caused between the attorney and the client by unpaid fees. Your clients will be happier, and therefore, more likely to recommend you to others. And you will save time because you won't have to chase after fees.

Offer to accept a credit card to bill against monthly, instead of a retainer fee. Additionally, offer on-line payment options. Your invoices will be paid an average of sixteen days earlier.

OPTIMIZE PRODUCTIVITY

Optimum productivity is another important aspect of running a business. Increase productivity by improving information flow. Don't waste valuable time inputting the same information into different software applications. Utilize apps like Google Apps, that automatically share information to all of your applications, and that are accessible from anywhere at any time. Use QuickBooks (I prefer to buy and download the program) for accounting and invoicing (including payroll, on-line payment, and credit card processing services), Harvest for time tracking, and Zapier, which allows QuickBooks and Harvest to communicate. Or use PC Law.

These programs work with Google Apps so that you only need to input your information once.

Use the note-taking app, Evernote. Share your notebooks with your employees, and install it on all your business devices. To keep it manageable, utilize tags rather than creating too many notebooks. For example, keep a notebook called "clients' correspondence," and then tag each piece of correspondence with the client's name.

You can also use Evernote as a paperless correspondence file. Hand-written notes can be scanned and saved to Evernote so that all of your notes are in one spot. This way, you aren't constantly searching for notes that could be saved in numerous different places. And, the notes themselves are searchable, which will save you time and money. You can easily set up a paperless e-mail file by integrating Evernote with Powerbot.

Avoid security issues caused by password theft by signing up for LastPass and using it to generate and store all of your passwords. Then enable two-factor authentication in as many places as possible.

Invest your time in creating quality web content, such as blog posts, rather than by spending money on pay-per-click advertising. Add a custom URL, custom permalinks, and custom Meta descriptions to improve search engine optimization. Google uses URL, permalinks, and Meta descriptions to determine the subject of your blog.

Also invest in professionally made web videos. To save money, use an independent videographer who works from his home rather than in a studio. Use your videos in conjunction with your blog posts.

Use your time more effectively. Ask each person in your office (including yourself!) to set aside a block of time each morning to read all of their e-mails in their inbox and papers in their paper inbox, and take action.

Avoid reading, setting aside, and then re-reading because that wastes time. Instead, rather than taking breaks in the middle of a task to read an e-mail you don't have time to answer, make time in your day to answer e-mails and accomplish the tasks associated with them. Not only will you save money, but your clients will be happier because their questions will be answered more rapidly. And cases will be completed more quickly, ensuring your clients' satisfaction and giving you more time to take on new ones.

Also, set a weekly meeting with your entire office to review your calendar for the upcoming week and set action items. Then, immediately follow through on the most pressing items before moving onto other tasks. This will reduce your stress because hearings, meetings, and deadlines won't surprise you.

Further, schedule a staff meeting once a month during which you audit the status of all of your files to determine what needs to be done. When you're finished auditing the file, and making sure that everything that could be accomplished actually has been, send the client a quick one-page letter or e-mail updating her as to the status of her case, informing her what you've done since the last audit period and what you'll be doing over the next audit period, and giving her your honest outlook as to the case.

Additionally, schedule a Friday or a Saturday every six months when you and your staff can complete nagging outstanding administrative tasks.

Finally, set regular office hours and keep them, even when you don't have appointments. And, when you're at work, work. If you need to take time for personal errands, make up for it later in the day. You'll get more accomplished, and your staff will be more productive, too.

Hire the Right Employees at the Right Times

Realize that you are only ready to hire an associate when that associate will generate more income than you are going to pay him. Hiring an employee should increase your profits. Don't hire someone to do the things you can't do or don't want to do. If you are unable to do something, you won't be able to supervise your associate or know whether they are performing a task correctly or efficiently. And you'll run the risk of committing malpractice. And if you're hiring someone simply because you don't want to do something or you want to take more time off, remember that you are a businessperson, which means sometimes you have to do things you don't want to do or work when you don't want to. It is part of being an entrepreneur, and it's what it takes to be successful.

When you do decide to hire someone, consider what it is you need so that you hire the right person. Don't hire a lawyer to do an assistant's job. Don't hire a salaried employee when you only need a contractor to perform ten hours of work a week.

Before you bring on the new person, be sure that procedures are in place to provide an environment in which the employee will be able to work independently in the role you need filled. Hire slowly and methodically so that you increase the chances that you hire the right person for the job who is proactive and diligent.

Once you have hired someone, take the time to train him and to ease him into his workload. You'll be more likely to retain him and more confident that he has the skills to do the job.

* * *

In short, before you hang your shingle, be sure that you understand what it takes to become a productive and effective businessperson. These tips will lead you on the right path to being a successful entrepreneur.

Define Your Personal Brand (Before You Begin Marketing II)

Your personal brand encapsulates the totality of the public's experiences when they interact with you. To develop your practice effectively and strategically, you must first define your personal brand. Your personal brand will then become the shorthand for you, your practice, who you are and what your practice offers the lay consumer, i.e. everything that you need to market yourself.

Start by thinking about yourself as a brand. Explore what makes you . . . well, *you*. What are your values? What drives your life? What makes you tick? What qualities do you consider when making crucial decisions? What is important to you? Why do you practice the type of law that you do? What do you want to be known for? What are your goals? What fuels your passion?

Be aware of who you are, as well as who you are not.

Once you have listed your core values, prioritize them. While your family and profession might both be important to you, if your family is more important, you won't be content with a career that keeps you from it, even if it is a rewarding one.

What are you passionate about? While your passions probably include some of your values, your passions are the activities that give you the most happiness and afford you the most satisfaction in your day-to-day life. While your values may include your family and maintaining a healthy lifestyle, your passion may be running races with your husband because that is the activity that intersects most with your values.

Next, determine your ideal traits. If this is difficult for you, look to those whom you admire, and consider what traits they exemplify that you emulate.

Now, how does the world see you? Once you have explored your values, passions, and ideal traits, discuss them with your closest family members and friends to ascertain whether they truly define how the world sees you. When building your brand, how the world perceives *you* is more important than how you perceive yourself.

And by the way, if the public does not perceive you as you would like, there is no time like the present to effectuate the necessary change.

So, if you want your brand to convey a defined message about who you are and the services you provide, make a conscious effort to display those traits for which you would like to be known. Reinvent yourself! And as long as you are consistent, it won't take long. Everything you do ultimately contributes to your personal brand.

Once you have defined it, ensure that the way you present yourself publicly, how you behave, your on-line presence, etc. are all consistent with your brand message. Be strategic about what you share and with whom you connect.

When reinventing yourself, be sure that you are doing so in a way that is true to who you really are. If you do not, you will be stained with the reputation of being a "fake," and it will be hard to regain that trust. Be clear about what you stand for, even if it is off-putting to some people.

Always strive for quality over quantity when communicating over social media. While the demands of social media can be overwhelming, it is better to post less often, but always in a thoughtful and entertaining way.

Shoot for consistency in the frequency of your posts.

And don't forget to come out from behind the computer, as well, so that you have a real self to go along with your virtual self.

Defining your personal brand is the foundation for all marketing and business development. Once you have clarified it, then your brand will become the shorthand for you, who you are, your practice, and the services your practice offers the consumer. This then becomes the crux upon which you build the rest of your marketing efforts.

Top Ten Marketing Mistakes Made by the Legal Professional

Not Marketing

There are five easily identifiable steps to your marketing plan. We will explore all of these further in both this chapter and later in the book, but for now, know that you should:

Pitch. Do you have clarity? Do you clearly articulate the value of the services you provide? Do you have a compelling answer to the question "What do you do?" An answer that invites questions? Clarity is the ability to communicate your message in a way that is convincing.

Word-of-mouth marketing is one of the most effective ways to grow your practice. Join groups. Attend seminars and trainings. Lecture. Write blogs. Tweet about all of it. Become an influencer or a champion in the realm in which you have chosen to focus your practice.

You provide a remarkable service. Accelerate awareness of who you are and the value of the services your firm provides, by attending events and by sharing with clarity.

Publish. Do you have authority in your profession? In your practice area? Does the public perceive you as the expert, as having the right answers? Credibility enables you to write clear and compelling blogs, articles, tweets, chapters, and books that people will read, relate to, and, perhaps most importantly, share with others.

You can't raise awareness and interest without establishing your credibility first. And you won't establish your credibility if you ignore the power of the written word, whether it's pen-and-paper or electronic.

Present. Are you invited to speak at trainings, at events, on podcasts, and on radio shows? Are you asked to interview on TV? Do people seek you out because of your ability to connect with a crowd? Coherence is your ability to communicate your vision persuasively to more than one person at a time.

Among other things, appear on radio, on podcasts, and on television. Call local professionals who have radio, podcast, or television shows, and offer to be a guest. Many of these local media talents are always looking for experts to help them fill airtime. Follow up on your press releases with radio and television marketing personnel.

Prepare your PowerPoints before you need them from articles and blogs you have written. Create a library of ten or twenty 60-minute PowerPoints that you can offer to present at the drop of a hat when you get that unexpected request to fill in for someone.

You can't raise awareness of who you are and interest in your services without communicating your vision to more than one person at a time. You will only reach that tipping point of raising awareness and interest in your community if you present powerfully and coherently.

Profile. Is your personal brand conspicuous, visible, and easily identified, both on-line and in traditional media? Do you take your ideas, your vision, and your cause "above the noise?" If not, why not?

Among other things, solicit and post written and video testimonials of satisfied clients on your website and on YouTube.

Be active on social media. You can't raise awareness of and interest in your practice without being visible and conspicuous. This means that you must go out of your way to ensure that your personal brand reflects both who you are and also your mission and your vision.

Partner. Are you connected with the other legal professionals in your community? With other providers who service the same clients that you do? Do others reach out to you to provide you with value because they perceive you to have value for *them*?

Construct your partnership pitch, taking exactly the same steps that you originally took to create your elevator pitch. But now your pitch is targeted at all of those possible compatriots you might want as referral partners, as mentors, as protégés, and as service partners. That also includes the independent contractor professionals who can help you with mastering the tools of marketing, such as the social media consultants, the website developers, the videographers, and the SEO experts, etc.

More importantly, what you begin to realize, as you become proficient at the first four fortes discussed above, is that potential partners will approach you. The question becomes whether you are able to distinguish the valuable partnerships from those that will provide you with no benefit.

MARKETING TOO BIG

The entire world or "everyone" is *not* your market. Define your ideal client profile. Understanding your ideal client will allow you to say the right thing to the right person at the right moment to convert him or his best friend or his daughter into a client.

Don't just think of the individual. Think of groups and the roles that people play, that they fit into.

And always keep in mind that, although you may market a specific type of practice area, that may not mean that you will not handle other legal matters. Have you heard of the gal who marketed her services as the *Nudist Realtor*? She specialized in buying and selling homes in nudist colonies. Did she *not* sell homes to people who wore clothes? Of course, she did. Her niche attracted clients, both in that niche and outside it. And she didn't turn down perfectly good customers just because they were wearing clothes, now did she?

This brings me to my next mistake.

Offering No Service Options

If appropriate, inform clients during your initial consultation that you offer a variety of services, including, for example, if true, unbundled services, and limited representation. You are willing to help on just one issue or one task. You are able to ghostwrite for them. You can review documents for them. Offer to be their coach and on-call for important meetings, like mediations and settlement conferences, or depositions. Attend sessions as a consultant, as a client resource rather than an advocate. Offer second opinions.

In fact, ensure that your staff also offers all of these possibilities to people who call for information. Your staff should be as conversant as are you about all of the process options that you can offer.

Ensure that all of these options are also clear on your website. Compare and contrast a full-service approach with a limited service approach, and be sure to discuss the risks and benefits of both with all of your potential clients.

Don't sell yourself short by offering only a Big Mac when it's just as easy for you to offer a Quarter Pounder, with or without cheese, with or without the Secret Sauce. Et Voila! Now you have service options.

Not Pitching Purposefully

Your quick pitch should be your most effective (and salient) form of permission marketing. Its sole purpose is to encourage your listener to ask you to "tell me more." When he does, he gives you permission to discuss your services in-depth with a participant (him!) who is now willing to listen.

Now that you have permission, identify exactly what service you provide; name it. Use clear and concise language that is easy to understand. Use adjectives and adverbs. Name the payoff for your clients. Explain why you care about offering this service.

Now pitch! Time yourself to no more than 30 seconds. Speak clearly so that you can be heard. Make sure that your pitch is conversational.

Smile. If you act as if you are enthusiastic, you will *be* enthusiastic.

Practice your pitch often. Finish it strong. If you are rushed, your all-important "memory hook" fades out in your haste to finish and you end up sounding like you're apologizing.

Avoid pitching to someone when one of you is rushed or distracted. If the timing is inappropriate, it won't matter how well you deliver your pitch.

People are influenced more by people to whom they feel connected. If you've shared a laugh or a story, or identified a common connection, your pitch is more likely to land with your audience.

Ensure that your pitch can be understood by anyone. Don't use jargon or acronyms and don't try to impress people with your insider lingo. Simplify!

Don't pitch anything you cannot deliver. For example, my office offers a valuable service, but we cannot promise a specific resolution when we tell someone we can get them divorced. So, do not ever leave people questioning your credibility to deliver the promised result.

Deliver your pitch with passion, grounded enthusiasm, and your own unique flair. Share your beliefs and your story so that people will remember who you are and what you stand for. It's not a great pitch if it's easily forgotten. The reason you're pitching is to engage others in helping you to spread the word that you are available to render your unique legal services, not simply so that they can see that you have things under control. You must know what you want from them and ask for it.

Pitch regularly. If you pitch powerfully repeatedly, you will achieve almost anything. But even a compelling pitch that you deliver only once a month will go nowhere fast. Pitch to yourself every time you brush your teeth, every time you get in the car, and every time you take your vitamins. Then pitch to those you meet every time you buy a cup of coffee at Starbucks, every time you check out at the grocery store, and every time you get on an elevator. I will bet that you sign a client within a month of first doing that, as a direct result.

NOT PUBLISHING PURPOSEFULLY

How many different venues can you publish in? The list these days is interminable. And your perfect client abides in at least one, if not several. If you don't publish, you ignore a way to establish your credibility and an easy way for your client to find you.

Blog, tweet, comment, write, and publish often. Construct an avatar of your perfect client or picture a real person whom you want your articles to reach. Identify the burning questions your avatar wants answered.

Every time you publish you should offer your unique take on a subject. There's no point in being a clone of an existing legal personality. Your perspective is yours alone. Keep in mind the specific next step that you want your avatar to take right after she finishes reading your article. Make sure to include that call to action in every piece you write.

Additionally, your website's design and content should consistently communicate your practice's overall brand image and messaging. Update your website frequently. The best way to enjoy repeat readers is to always offer new and meaningful entries. Invite your avatar to leave comments by posing questions to him. Be sure to respond to his comments. Promote your blog and develop a community around it. Research new tools and features that may enhance your avatar's experiences. Let your personality shine through in your articles.

NOT PRESENTING PURPOSEFULLY

Show an authentic interest in those with whom you converse. Listen actively, and ask questions. Connect with them, and then follow up relentlessly. Schedule lunches; send materials you discussed, etc.

Appear on radio and television. Don't forget to reach out to podcast producers, as well. Call local professionals who have radio, podcast, or television shows, and offer to be a guest. Again, follow up on your press releases with radio, podcast, and television marketing personnel.

You raise awareness and interest by communicating your vision to more than one person at a time, through presentations and spirited discussions. And you will only reach that tipping point of raising awareness and interest in your community if you present often, both powerfully and coherently.

Not Working Your Profile Purposefully

What is your vision? What is your mission? You should be able to explain them to potential clients, friends, family, and colleagues, to everyone.

We are a technologically advanced society. The vast majority of American adults own a smartphone, a computer, and/or a tablet. (In fact, so do their kids!) Most Americans are members of social networking websites like LinkedIn, Facebook, Twitter, and Instagram. It is a mistake to fail to use this technology to maximize your exposure of your brand, your vision, and your mission. To market your services.

So, of course, you post. But you must also maintain an awareness of what the current trends are, and the way this generation receives information and markets, as well as what's acceptable for lawyers to do. For example, today, as I pen this chapter, you should be soliciting and posting written and video testimonials of satisfied clients on your website and on YouTube.

Not Partnering

Attend events. Introduce yourself to everyone you meet. Give your business card to anyone who requests it. Use your pitch. Share your stories when you do. Make friends. Ask for business cards from those with whom you wish to follow up. Follow up and invite your new friends to lunch or for a cup of coffee.

Continue to attend seminars and trainings. Not only will you learn new skills and hone old ones, you will meet new professionals and build your relationships with professionals whom you already know.

While it is important to meet as many people as possible, focus on really getting to know a few people. Referrals result most often from established relationships. People refer to professionals whom they know, like, and trust.

Offer to present at events you've attended in the past.

Another great way to really get to know a small group of professionals is to organize a seminar, a training, a workshop, or a CLE event yourself. Form a training committee or a speakers' bureau. Not only will you build relationships with those on your committee, but you'll strengthen your relationships with the more established professionals who speak at the training.

These are just a few examples of how you must partner to help you market.

No Follow Up

Speaking of partnering, let your clients know regularly and often how much you appreciate them. Let them know what other services you provide that may benefit them. Do a good job for them, and remind them to refer their friends to you. Don't be afraid to ask for referrals; if you don't ask, believe it or not, it might not occur to them that you would appreciate the referral!

Build a relationship with your clients. Become a resource or a trusted advisor. Anticipate their needs, and be proactive. Also, know who your key referral service providers are. Turn new clients into loyal clients.

PITCH

INTRODUCTION TO PITCH FORTES

Pitching does not come naturally to most of us. As lawyers, we don't consider ourselves salespeople, even though part of running a successful practice involves marketing to potential clients and to other professionals ourselves and what we can uniquely offer.

This section will teach you how to become more comfortable with your pitching. You will learn the different types of pitches, as well as appropriate times to use each type of pitch and appropriate people to whom to pitch. You will not only learn how to write and perfect your pitches, but also how to become so comfortable giving them that they no longer feel rehearsed. You will learn tips to become a better pitcher, like the importance of practicing your pitch every day. You will also learn errors to avoid when pitching, like pitching to an unenthusiastic audience or to someone who is in a hurry.

As you read, I encourage you to start thinking about your pitches. Once you have completed this section, write them down. Learn them. Practice them on your friends and family, asking for feedback each time. Once you are happy with them, practice them daily, and pitch as often as you can, as is appropriate. You'll have more new clients and professional relationships in no time.

Pitch Basics

- ✓ Elevator/quick pitch (15 to 30 seconds)
- ✓ Social pitch (one to two minutes)
- ✓ Media pitch (five minutes)

Quick Pitch

Your quick pitch is your most poignant form of permission marketing. Its sole purpose is to get the listener to say "tell me more." When he does, you have permission to explain in depth the value of your services to a now willing participant, a rapt audience.

1. Your claim to fame: what service do you provide?
2. The problem and your solution: what pain or suffering does your service alleviate?
3. Your mission: why do you care about your service? What is your larger goal?
4. Practice/revise/practice again.

Pitching Tips

- Pitch often and to those whom you don't know.
- Determine who your ideal listener is, and craft your pitch based on what you would want him to know.
- Make it conversational and unique.
- Consider making predictions about what the future holds or busting a popular myth.
- Include case studies and personal stories.
- Time yourself to no more than 30 seconds (65-95 words, depending on how fast you speak).
- Include a call to action. What do you want the listener to do once they have heard your pitch?
- Create a memory hook that appeals to all of the basic senses. Or better yet, make people laugh. (*With* you, not *at* you!)
- Practice! Practice! Practice! Know your pitch by heart.

- Project. Speak clearly so that you can be heard.
- Smile. Act enthusiastic and you'll be enthusiastic. If you don't show us that you believe in what you do, neither will we.
- Finish strong; if you rush, your memory hook fades in your haste to finish and ends up sounding like an apology . . . not good!
- Create a version of your pitch that can be tweeted (140 characters or less).
- Train your staff to pitch effectively.

SOCIAL PITCH

This is what you use at the cocktail party and at the networking event. What is in your social pitch?

1. Your name and what you do;
2. Your authority;
3. The problem/pain;
4. Your solution/gain;
5. Your authentic why (why do you do it?); and
6. Your reputation (what your clients say about you).

SOCIAL PITCHING TIPS

- Deliver it at least three times a day.
- Teach it to your staff and your family.
- Deliver it while driving your car or in line at the grocery store.
- Watch and listen to how it lands and revise it again.
- Tape it to your bathroom mirror (deliver it three times before you leave the bathroom in the mornings) and to your refrigerator door (practice it at least once before you allow yourself to open the fridge). Keep a copy on your dashboard. (Only refer to it at stoplights.) Learn it by heart.
- Deliver it to your prospective clients. Deliver it to your referral sources. Deliver it at events. Deliver it to other professionals. Deliver it to anyone who will listen.

SOCIAL PITCHING ERRORS

- Pitching at the wrong time or in the wrong place, as when the listener is rushed, distracted, or feels that it is an inappropriate time for you to deliver your pitch.
- Pitching before you have taken the time to establish rapport by sharing a joke, a laugh, a personal story, etc.
- Pitching in a confusing, unclear manner filled with jargon.
- Pitching before you have established any credibility.
- Not being extraordinary or passionate about what you are pitching.

- Forgetting to include a call to action.
- Not pitching often enough.

What's the universal constant in the pitch of the legal professional? People should understand that they have a choice, that there is a conscious decision to make about which path to take, that there are many options and that you can counsel them best about which options to choose.

Where do you pitch and how do you deliver your pitch? The answer is through networking, also known as word-of-mouth marketing.

1. First, provide a remarkable service.
2. Then, accelerate awareness of who you are and the value your services provide, by attending events and sharing.
3. When you attend events, show an authentic interest in those with whom you converse. How? Listen actively; ask questions. Connect. Find out how you can help those with whom you connect.
4. Then follow up. Relentlessly. Schedule lunch; send materials you discussed, etc.

What's the goal of such marketing? Referrals. Referrals result most often from established relationships. People refer to professionals they know, like, and trust. So, build mutually beneficial relationships. "How can I help you and your business?" "Tell me more about your referral sources. Do I know any to whom I can refer you? Can I introduce you?"

Schedule a one-to-one with each person with whom you connect. Discuss his business, your practice, how he can help you, and how you can help him. Show a genuine interest in him and he will respond with a genuine interest in you.

Identify your best referral sources. Ask how you can help them. How can you refer them business?

How do you find new referral sources? Make a list of organizations in which you might have an interest and that it might make sense to join. These might be:

- Service organizations
- Charitable organizations
- Business oriented groups
- Professional organizations
- Referral organizations
- Religious organizations
- Other organizations and groups

Then what?

- Join

- Volunteer for a committee
- Volunteer for a position
- Host a meeting
- Fill a gap, if you see one
- Present
- Lead
- Mentor

SOCIAL PITCHING

Now that I've outlined how the social pitch is composed, let's review mine. Can you identify the separate elements? As you do, consider how it would change if *you* were the one delivering it.

> I am Joryn Jenkins. I help people divorce each other without destroying their families or their finances.
>
> I've been practicing law for 37 years. During that time, I've published extensively, including my books, *War or Peace* and *I Never Saw My Father Again*. I've received an award given only in the United States Supreme Court to one person once a year.
>
> Divorce is terrifying. There are so many questions! "How do I tell my spouse?" "What will happen to my kids?" "How much will it going to cost?" "How long will it take?"
>
> I solve that problem by offering an alternative to the conventional courtroom divorce. It costs less and it takes less time. You make the decisions, not some judge who doesn't know you or your kids, or share your values. And it protects your relationships with the people you care about: your children, your friends, your neighbors . . . and, yes, your soon-to-be-ex.
>
> When I was seven, my parents divorced. My mother loaded us kids into the van and moved us three thousand miles away. I never saw my father again.
>
> I don't want to see that happen to other children . . . to other families.
>
> I am known for helping my clients restructure their families, not destroy them. I'm Joryn Jenkins. I'm a lawyer . . . for families.

This is an example of a cocktail party pitch. Pitch is important, because it communicates how you can help others and what makes you unique from all the other people providing the same service. Pitch is also important, because it communicates your passion, your vision, and your mission.

There are more than three types of pitches, but these three are the ones you need to start with. There is the "elevator" pitch, the "cocktail party" pitch, and the "press" pitch. For those of us who are more matured in our marketing efforts, we might also create a partnership pitch, for example.

Do you clearly articulate the value of the services you provide? Do you have a compelling answer to the question "What do you do?" One that invites questions? Clarity is the ability to communicate your message in a way that convinces.

The elevator pitch's sole purpose is to plant a seed with the listener that will encourage him to ask questions. Timing is important. Thirty seconds is the general rule, which translates to 65-95 words.

Think about it. Most of us simply say, when asked what they do for a living, "I'm a lawyer." That was my "pitch" for years and years. The obvious response was always, "That's nice." Any possible conversation usually came to a screaming halt. A dead end to the discussion.

Once I realized how crucial it was that I answered this question in a way to invite discussion, I morphed my elevator pitch. So now I say, "I help people divorce each other without destroying their families or their finances." And, without fail, folks tilt their heads, quizzically. And then they ask me to tell them more.

You will use your elevator pitch in the least likely of places. One day, I was waiting in line at Sam's Club to make a return, because my husband hates to return purchases. (He had accidentally bought the long, flat boxes of tissues, not the square little boxes that fit in our decorative dispensers at home.)

Bored to death on a line that might as well have stretched to the moon, I was standing behind this guy who was dressed head-to-toe in Gator garb. He was blue and orange all over! I commented (not my most inspired opening, by the way), "Oh, my gosh, you're a Gator, aren't you?"

He responded, clearly tickled to have someone to talk to, "No, no. But my daughter is a double Gator. Undergrad and law!"

Of course, he asked me what I do. I wasn't dressed like a lawyer. I certainly had no makeup on and I just as surely was wearing jeans and sandals, my standard shopping-at-Sam's garb. It was early. I'm not sure that I had even showered yet that day.

But I gave him my elevator pitch. Then my social pitch. One thing led to another, and, two days later, his daughter was in my office asking me for professional services with respect to the legal matter in which she was embroiled, her own divorce.

So, in addition to the elevator pitch, there is also the cocktail party pitch. It is longer, a total of about two minutes, or 260-380 words, although, in a perfect world, you will never deliver it in one lengthy spiel. This social pitch is built of several components: your name, what you do, your perfect avatar client's problem, and your solution, i.e. what pain or suffering your service alleviates, and what end result people will get when they use your service. You should also explain why you are passionate about the service you perform for folks. And you should close with your reputation, i.e. what you are known for.

Once you've crafted your social pitch, the next important step is to practice it so that it becomes ingrained, so that you can give it with confidence. During my daily drive to work, I typically run through my social pitch at least three times in 12 minutes. I used to have it pinned up to the mirror in my bathroom. Before I had it memorized, I would practice it every morning three times before I left the bathroom. (Yes, I probably spend too much time in front of the mirror. But I'm a girl.)

Because practicing it is so important, where else can you practice your pitch? You can pitch pretty much anywhere . . . at McDonald's, at the grocery store, at church, at your bar association, at your children's school, etc.

While pitching can be done anywhere, anytime, you should take care to avoid the most common pitfalls. There *are* some wrong times or places to make a pitch. Do not make a pitch when you have no rapport with the listener. Do not use jargon while making your pitch. Do not make a pitch when you have no credibility because you cannot deliver what you promise. Don't be boring; failing to deliver your pitch with passion is a big mistake. Not personalizing your pitch to your listener is another pitfall.

Finally, inconsistency is a huge danger for pitch delivery. If you pitch anything passionately 1,000 times, you can achieve almost anything. But even a compelling pitch that only comes out of your mouth once a month will fizzle. *Pitch every day.*

How to improve your pitch:

- Clearly understand the value of the services you offer and the problems you can solve.
- Write your pitch down, and learn it by heart.
- Create a version of your pitch that can be Tweeted (140 characters or less).
- Pitch to people deliberately and specifically.
- Pitch as often as possible to people you don't know.
- Train your support staff to pitch their version of your pitch.

When crafting your pitch, consider who your listener is. Construct an avatar of your perfect listener or even picture a real person whom you would like to reach.

Once you have constructed your avatar, think about what it is that he wants to know. What is his big, burning question?

Be sure that your pitch positions you in a positive light and that you are attracting the sort of client you want.

Your pitch should clarify how what you offer is different from what other service providers offer. It should describe your unique take on things; there is no point in being a clone of an existing influencer or champion in your profession or your practice area.

Be clear as to the desired action you want your listener to take.

Now let's craft your personal social pitch; this is what you use at the cocktail party, at the flea market, and at the networking event. I've even given my pitch, and brought in a new client, at a garage sale! Let's start with a simple outline:

1) Your name and what you do;
2) Your authority;
3) The problem/pain;
4) The solution/gain;
5) Your authentic why (why do you do it?); and
6) Your reputation (what do your clients say about you?).

Here is an example of a pitch outline designed for a lawyer. Pick and choose the elements that work for you and see what you get:

- Introduction.
- Famous person quote.
- Your background.
- Your name.
- Who you are; establish your credibility.
  - How many years in practice?
  - Education?
  - Experience?
  - Publications? Books?
  - Teaching?
  - Speaking?
  - Another claim to fame?
  - Joke - laugh at yourself.
  - Namedrop.
  - Quote statistics about your successful cases.
  - Use your passion/enthusiasm.
  - Don't be afraid to brag, but do it with humility.
  - Employ adjectives and adverbs to bring your passion alive.

- Define the problem that you are trying to fix. Identify three or four facets of it. (People can easily recall just 3-4 items, and no more than that.)
  - Make people aware of the problem.
  - Make people afraid of the problem.
  - Plant the seed of doubt.
  - Personal story?

- What's the solution? Identify three or four characteristics of it.
  - What's your vision?
  - What would the world look like if . . . ?
  - Shotgun benefits?

- What do you want from your listener? What's your "ask?"
  - Referrals?
  - Speaking opportunities?
  - Connections?
  - Partnerships?

- How do you present?
  - Memorize it.
  - How do you close after each piece?
  - Do you have a tag line? A memory hook?
  - State the name of your business again at the close.
  - Remember that gestures help to tell the story.

Now, let's review the pitch basics. Where do you pitch and how do you deliver your pitch? The easy answer is "Everywhere and all the time." The more organized and planned answer (again) is through networking, or "word-of-mouth marketing."

1) First, provide a full and remarkable solution.
2) Then, accelerate awareness of who you are and the value of the services that you provide, by attending events and sharing with the folks you meet there.
3) When you do, show an authentic interest in those with whom you converse. How? Listen actively; ask questions. Connect. Find out how you can help those with whom you do connect.
4) Then follow up. Relentlessly. Schedule lunch, e-mail materials you may have discussed, send a written thank-you note (very unusual these days and therefore noteworthy), etc.

What's your goal for such marketing? Rarely do we hope to land a consult with the person with whom we connect, although that does, of course, occasionally happen. But, regardless of that possibility, we simply aim for referrals. Referrals result most often from established relationships. People most often refer to lawyers they know, like, and trust.

And you don't just ask for help. You offer it, as well. "Tit for tat," as my grandma used to say. So, you build mutually beneficial relationships. "How can I help you and *your* business?" "Tell me more about *your* referral sources. Do I know anyone I might be able to introduce you to?"

Schedule a one-to-one with each person with whom you spend any time at these events. Discuss his business, your practice, how he can help you, and how you can help him. Try to figure out why *he* should care about your practice.

Identify your best referral sources, your first responders. Schedule some "social" time with these folks, as well. Perhaps a coffee or a glass of wine. Ask how you can help them. How can you refer them business?

How do you find new referral sources? Let's review this:

- Service organizations
- Charitable organizations
- Business oriented groups
- Professional organizations
- Referral organizations
- Religious organizations
- Other organizations and groups

Then what?

- Join
- Volunteer for a committee
- Volunteer for a position
- Host a meeting
- Fill a gap
- Present
- Lead
- Mentor

Now that you've crafted your initial cocktail party pitch (remember, it will morph as you watch it land and realize that you can hone it still more), let's review these pitching tips:

- Memorize your pitch.
- Time yourself to no more than two minutes (260-380 words).
- Now you can make it conversational and practice saying it often.
- Practice! Practice! Practice! Deliver it at least three times a day. Deliver it while driving your car or on line at the grocery. Tape it to your bathroom mirror and to your refrigerator door. Tape it to your front door and deliver it at least once on your way out in the morning.
- Watch how it lands. How does your audience respond? Do you need to clarify, amend, explain . . . ? Rewrite it again.
- Project. Speak clearly so that you are heard. Remember: body language is effective internally, as well as externally.
- Smile. Act enthusiastic and you'll *be* enthusiastic. If you don't show us that you believe in what you do, neither will we.
- Finish strong; if you rush, your memory hook fades in your haste to finish and it ends up sounding like an apology . . . not good!
- Teach it to your staff and your family. Your kids should know it as well as you do.
- Deliver it to your prospective clients. Deliver it at events. Deliver it

to your referral sources. Deliver it to everyone.

Now let's review the most common errors that professionals make when they pitch:

- They pitch at the wrong time or in an inappropriate place;
- They lack rapport with their listener;
- They lack clarity in their pitch;
- They lack credibility;
- Their pitch is not extraordinary;
- They forget to ask, their call to action, so they don't get; or
- Their pitch is internally inconsistent.

So, what's the first, most crucial step to raising the public perception of who you are and the value of the services you provide? The answer is "pitching!"

Now get out there and start pitching!

An important aspect of pitching a consult is the ability to appeal to the personal interests of your potential client and to be able to explain complex concepts in a way that he will understand. Before you begin to pitch yourself and your approach to your law practice to a potential client, take a moment to really see who your audience is. What is his nationality? How is he dressed? Does he have any interests that are immediately obvious? What are his passions? Observe him. You can often learn a lot about what is really important to a person just by taking a moment to look and listen. Once you have accomplished that, you can stress the aspects of your pitch that will appeal to him, in particular. You can also use analogies that he will understand better than others, as in the tale below, when I had to explain the collaborative approach to divorce to my Korean consult.

As you read my story, think of your own practice area. How do you explain what you do to prospective clients, without using legalese?

The Aikido Divorce
(Pitch Your Consult I)

Have you ever watched a martial arts movie and thought, "There is no way this small dude could ever beat that mountain of a guy?" Well, you're not alone. But due to precise and well-practiced technique, David is able to topple Goliath with intelligence and anticipation that more than adequately counters power and brute force. In this way, the collaborative divorce process is superior to the conventional courtroom divorce process in knocking down the frightening monster we all know as "divorce."

Collaborative divorce is similar to Aikido, a Japanese martial art. 'Aiki' refers to the principle of blending with a partner's movements for the purpose of minimizing harm to all: 'ai' means 'joining, unifying, or combining'; 'ki' refers to 'spirit or energy'; and 'do' denotes 'path.' Thus, Aikido translates as the 'Way of Combining Forces' or the 'Way of Harmony.'

In Aikido, one applies aiki by, first, understanding the rhythm and intent of others to, and second, finding the optimal position and timing to connect and diffuse the conflict. It was developed in the early 20th century by Morihei Uyeshiba, is based on harmony and love, and is rooted firmly in the eastern philosophical notions of dualism and polarity.

I had a client whose story illustrated how closely Aikido resembles the collaborative divorce process. I remember the sun pushing through the blinds, illuminating the brown leather couch in my office, and casting a diagonal shadow on the cushions. It was a hot summer afternoon when my consult walked through the door, with a hint of anxiety he was unable to hide playing in his eyes.

"My name's Joryn. It's a pleasure to meet you." I greeted him, as I rose from my seat, looked him in those eyes, and reached for his hand.

"I'm pleased to make your acquaintance. My name's Jung Shin." He inclined his torso slightly, over our clasped hands. I realized that he was bowing. Compared to American standards, he was a short man, but amongst his Korean counterparts, at 5'8", he was fairly average.

He was slender, as well, but, by the way his clothing hung on him, I could tell that he had recently lost a significant amount of weight. I later learned that over the prior six months, due to the stress of the breakup of his relationship, he had lost 35 pounds. He was terrified that he might be seriously ill, but his physician assured him that, beyond the stress, there was nothing medically wrong with him.

Having been diagnosed with juvenile diabetes in my thirties (go figure!) during an especially stressful time in my life, I discussed with him my concerns that, even though his weight loss was just caused by stress, that stress could lead to other major health issues if he was not careful. Divorce is one of the most stressful life experiences one will endure, but there are ways to reduce the stress significantly.

My assistant had already offered him something to drink, so I gestured invitingly toward the couch. "Please have a seat and tell me about your situation," I said, while settling on the armchair facing him.

"Yes." He sat, with a quick, single nod.

"My name's Shin," he repeated. "My wife and I have been married for nine years, but lately, it hasn't been working out. And now she's told me that she wants a divorce."

He continued, "I came from Korea at 15 with nothing but a suitcase, $96, a lot of determination, and a black belt in Aikido."

I nodded my head approvingly and continued to listen.

He went on, looking down at his clasped hands. "When I was 35, I married a Korean woman who was ten years younger than I am. We've never had children. Now my wife tells me she wants a divorce. We have a house with a mortgage. We each have a business with quite a bit of debt associated with them, especially hers. We each have a car, some bank and retirement accounts, and some personal loans. I really don't know what to do," he added in a subdued voice. He heaved a sigh, and then concluded by saying, "Also, I don't understand divorce. Can you explain what happens next?" He finally looked up, waiting for my response.

"Of course." I proceeded to explain the traditional courtroom process, as well as the various courtless options that my office recommends. When I arrived at the collaborative practice alternative, I continued, "My husband is a black belt in Aikido, as well, so here's an analogy that may help explain the collaborative divorce option." I smiled, hopeful that I could explain it in terms he would appreciate.

"Collaborative divorce is like aikido where conventional courtroom divorce is like karate," I continued passionately, "Aikido is more reciprocal and unifying, rather than karate, which is more forceful and adversarial."

Although he looked at me with a slight frown, puzzled, he nodded, clearly interested in hearing more.

I continued, "In keeping with the tenets of aikido, collaborative divorce is a far more unifying form of peaceful negotiations, whereas courtroom divorce is a more singular form of combat designed to defeat one's opponent thoroughly."

After another hour of exploring the benefits of collaborative divorce, Shin suddenly rose from the couch, leaving only a slight imprint where he had been sitting. I rose, as well. He smiled, somewhat shyly, I thought.

"Let's go collaborative!" He decided. "I hope that my wife will agree."

I was pleased that Shin wished to proceed collaboratively because I truly felt that it was the best divorce option for him, especially considering his stress-induced medical concerns. The decision would now rest with his wife. It takes two to collaborate, and she had already retained counsel who I knew to be a well-respected trial lawyer, and who had already filed a petition for divorce.

Nevertheless, I had recently seen her attorney, Pam Gold, at a collaborative training and had later noticed her at a couple of collaborative practice group meetings. I passed this information along to Mr. Shin. He shared with me that the Korean community in town is extremely tightly knit, and that he planned to talk to a few of the "movers and shakers" (my words, not his) that his wife was liable to listen to for advice, to seek their support in getting her on board.

I called Pam, and unsurprisingly, was unable to get further than her receptionist. I left a detailed message, explaining that I had been retained by Mr. Shin in his divorce, and that, although his wife had already filed, I wanted to speak with Pam about the possibility of proceeding collaboratively.

When Pam did not return my call for several days, I began to lose hope that she and her client would agree to the collaborative process option. However, she finally did call. I was pleasantly surprised by her out-of-the-box contrition. She apologized profusely, "I am so sorry to just now be returning your call, but I have been out of town helping my mother. She's very sick," she explained.

I replied without thinking, "Oh, I understand. My father-in-law has been having his own health issues recently, and, thank goodness, he lives nearby, so I can jump on the interstate and be there in 20 minutes to help." I proceeded quickly to business. "Have you had an opportunity to consider the possibility of proceeding collaboratively in the Shin divorce?"

She responded, "To be honest, I hadn't really until you suggested it. I guess I'm still thinking like a trial lawyer. But, I recently completed the collaborative training and, although I realize that I am known as a bit of a bulldog, as I get older, and see what my mother is going through, I am looking for ways to eliminate stress in my life. Collaborative practice may be the answer I'm looking for," she concluded.

I asked, "Have you had a chance yet to work on a case collaboratively?"

"I have not," she was quick to respond, "but I am excited by the opportunity, and I hope that you can teach an old dog some new tricks. But, now that my client has already petitioned for divorce, is collaborative even a possibility for this couple?"

"Oh yes," I hastened to explain, "We just file the fully executed participation agreement and notify the clerk that the case should be transferred from the litigation track to the collaborative track. Of course, we could also file a stipulation to abate the proceedings." I realized that she had not been around for long, so I clarified, "Chief Judge Ramirez has been very supportive of our practice group's efforts to spread the word. Once the Court is aware that we are proceeding collaboratively, the clerk will cancel the case management conference that was set when the petition was filed and will not schedule any more hearings until we advise it otherwise."

Pam chewed on that. "Well, I will certainly discuss this possibility with Kikyo Shin, and I'll let you know what she says as soon as I can."

This was good news. "Great!" I replied and figured I'd have a few days to wait. I e-mailed Mr. Shin, and went back to work.

Less than a day later, Pam called to let me know that her client was a go, and we discussed which neutrals to use and when to schedule the first meetings. I was grateful that Pam agreed to use two neutrals, both of whom had had plenty of collaborative experience. I hoped that they would be able to offset her own inexperience and tendency to be overly aggressive.

The first team meeting was fairly typical, with the team reviewing the participation agreement with the clients, and the participants signing it, until we moved on to temporary relief matters. It was at this point that Pam allowed the litigator in her take over. She was adamant that her client needed $1,000 monthly alimony despite that Kikyo herself didn't seem to feel the need for it, and had earned more than my client in the years leading up to the divorce.

It wasn't long before the facilitator jumped in, calling for a break. She made a point to speak with both attorneys privately so that the clients would not realize that anything was amiss, but when we all returned, Pam's behavior was markedly changed. I couldn't tell if her client noticed her transformation, but she was no longer taking positions and grandstanding. Instead, she was actively listening, asking appropriate questions, and, when the meeting concluded, the participants had agreed to waive alimony altogether.

During the professionals' debrief, Pam apologized for how she had acted initially. She explained that she was having a hard time with the paradigm shift from trial lawyer to collaborative lawyer, and she thanked our facilitator for pulling her aside to remind her of her role. I complimented her on listening to the facilitator's advice and modifying her approach so quickly and appropriately. Because of it, we made good progress during the first meeting.

The second full team meeting ran more smoothly as Pam appeared to be getting the hang of the process. The clients had more debt than assets; that was the major issue in their divorce. As is the Korean way, they had taken out several private loans to start their businesses, primarily for Kikyo's spa and salon. They had also defaulted on the mortgage for the real property where her business was located, and several non-Korean creditors had obtained final judgments against them. Some of these debts were in Kikyo's name alone, but Jung had also signed for some of them. In Florida, because the clients had incurred these debts during their marriage, a judge would likely have split them equally between the two of them. But because we were proceeding collaboratively, we were not bound by that legality.

Nevertheless, Kikyo wanted Jung to take on most of the debt. It was our financial neutral who was finally able to get her to see the inequity in this. "Kikyo," she asked, "what were these loans used for?"

Kikyo begrudgingly responded, "To set up my spa."

"And," Kendra continued reasonably, "are you still running your spa?"

"Yes."

"Are you receiving income from your spa?"

"Yes."

"Do you feel it's unfair to have to share any of that income with Mr. Shin after the divorce?"

"Yes."

"Then," Kendra reasoned, "is it fair for Mr. Shin to take on a majority of these debts?"

Kikyo thought for a few moments before unhappily concluding, "I guess not."

Jung did agree to take a few of the debts, mainly because they were owed to members of his church, he did not believe that Kikyo would actually ever repay them, and he wanted to ensure that they were paid.

With the debt issues resolved, the participants were able to quickly resolve the other minor issues in their divorce in just the two meetings. If the clients had litigated the case, they would have spent tens of thousands of dollars litigating alimony and debt distribution, and likely would have arrived at a similar result.

Instead, Shin and his wife were able to amicably split up their assets and debts. By divorcing collaboratively, they avoided the emotional and financial maelstrom that a traditional courtroom divorce causes, along with the unfulfilled expectations that protracted litigation sets up.

Pam and I met for a glass of wine after the entire collaborative team attended the final evidentiary hearing with the Shins. She shared with me then that Kikyo had been visited by the elders in her church, who had explained the collaborative process to her and why it was so much better for the divorcing couple, even when there were no children, and why it was better for their entire community. That was why she had accepted the collaborative proposal when we had offered it.

"Were you sorry that she agreed to go collaborative?" I asked Pam.

"Absolutely not," she didn't hesitate. "I've been in practice 30 years and it was the best divorce experience I've had to date. I'm looking forward to the next one!"

I didn't tell Pam that I had met with the elders in the Shins' Korean church last year, when I had presented *What is Collaborative Divorce and Why Should You Care?* in my efforts to spread the word to the community's first responders when it comes to divorce.

* * *

Keep in mind that you must ensure you speak a language that your consult understands in order to properly pitch your practice to him. And it's not always a question of French or English, Korean or Japanese. Pitch the person, not just the benefits your services can provide to him.

Now that you have written your pitch, you have weighed all of the relative benefits that your legal services solution offers to potential clients, and you want to include them in your consult pitch. If there are a number of benefits, you may want to limit your pitch to exploring the one or two benefits that really speak to the consult sitting in your conference room.

But how do you actually present that pitch?

VISION PROCESSING (PITCH YOUR CONSULT II)

"You never get a second chance to make a good first impression." In fact, you only have 20 seconds to reduce your consult's anxiety and create interest. So, when marketing your practice, it is important to open with a statement that will make an impact and encourage your prospective client to want to hear more. This is why developing and perfecting your elevator pitch is so important.

But once you've been granted that opening, that interview, that opportunity, you should utilize the 30-60 minutes that you have as effectively as possible.

Preparation and practice are imperative before you speak with a potential client or referral source. What problem does she have that can you fix? Why should she care about what you have to say? What questions might she ask you? Prior to meeting with her, have your answers to these questions ready. Rather than trying to "sell" her on retaining you, share your passion for your practice. You will avoid coming across as a sleazy, used car salesman, and your enthusiasm will be contagious.

Part of preparing for your conversation with your prospect is learning as much as possible about him. What is his passion? What problem does he have that you can fix? What common interests do you share? What contacts do you have in common that could vouch for you and your credibility? What stories should you share about your past successes? Consider providing a list of references of other professionals, as well as testimonials from your clients.

The three phases of diagnostic exploration are 1) diagnosing the reasons for the issue, 2) exploring the impact of the issue on other individuals, and 3) visualizing how your capabilities can provide solutions to the issue. Each phase consists of initial questions to encourage the prospect to open up to you, controlling questions to keep him focused by seeking specific information, and confirming, by reframing questions to reiterate what he said and ensure that you heard and understood him correctly.

Initial questions are open-ended, non-threatening inquiries that invite the prospect to talk freely and make him feel that he controls the conversation. These questions are best asked at the beginning of the consultation to put the prospect at ease.

Control questions are those that do not invite the prospect to embellish his responses. Usually a simple "yes," "no," or other one-word responses are sufficient. Thus, control questions put you back in control of the conversation.

Confirming questions affirm that you understand the prospect and can be used to rectify any misunderstandings. They are also used to demonstrate your empathy and your expertise.

For all types of questions, keep it simple. Basic questions will generally elicit better responses than complex questions.

Once you have fully prepared for your meeting, show your prospect that you respect him and his time by arriving early, dressing appropriately, and being prepared. Use your active listening skills to diagnose the reasons for his issue. Adapt your pitch based on what the prospect tells you. Don't just provide a cookie cutter, one-sided speech. Instead, establish a rapport by listening to your prospect. Engage in an interactive dialogue with him and explain the purpose of your conversation.

Identify the reasons for his pain and how much each reason is contributing to his pain. Then, delve deeper by exploring the impact of this matter on his loved ones. Ask who will be impacted, and then confirm what you have heard.

Next, the vision processing begins. Repeat his needs and vividly explain how you can solve his problem. Open this part of the conversation by asking for his dream outcome.

Detail the fit of your firm with the client. Share your client testimonials and success stories. Then, confirm whether he believes you could help him.

Throughout your conversation, ask questions that should cause your prospect to answer "yes." By doing so, it will be easier for him to respond affirmatively that he would like to proceed with retaining you.

Pitch your consult carefully. Plan ahead. Maximizing the first impression you make is key to marketing, and, by following these steps, you will sign more clients.

SUPPORT STAFF PITCH

As the first contact or gatekeepers to your firm, your support staff plays a vital role in pitching your practice to potential clients. They are the first ones with whom potential clients speak, and therefore, they provide those all-important first impressions. Your receptionists should be caring, sympathetic people who are willing to take some time with each caller, understanding that the first call to a law firm is often an emotional and difficult step for most people to take.

Provide your staff with a script of how they should respond to callers' frequently asked questions. Once a month, listen to one of their calls so that you are confident that they are providing the information accurately and in the manner and with the tone that you would like.

My support staff has been wonderful in first explaining the various divorce options to callers and convincing them to come in to hear more from our attorneys. A caller recently cold-called our office. My receptionist so accurately and enthusiastically explained the divorce process options that, when I sat down to actually do the consultation, he interrupted me with specific questions about how a collaborative divorce worked. By the time I spoke with him, because of the information that my receptionist had already provided to him, he had researched collaborative practice and was ready to proceed collaboratively in his divorce. My receptionist certainly made my job easy! This is your end goal in training your staff to deliver your legal services pitch.

On another occasion, my paralegal was attending a Pilates mat class, and another student complained that her husband had just filed for divorce. The woman was distraught; she fretted aloud that her husband would drag her through the court system and try to take "full custody" of their children. Apparently, she had been divorced before and that is what her first husband had put her through.

After listening for some time and letting the woman vent her frustrations, my paralegal told her how sorry she was, that she worked for a family law attorney, and that a litigated war was not her only option. By this time, the entire mat class was listening with rapt attention. My paralegal, who had just attended an introductory training on the collaborative divorce process, knowledgeably explained the various options available to folks considering divorce, stressing that the best interests of the children, rather than destroying the other spouse, should be at the forefront of the couple's thoughts. She clarified that the collaborative team would make sure that the primary interests of both spouses were met and that the spouses would learn invaluable communication and co-parenting skills that would help them going forward and reduce the possibility of post-judgment litigation. At the end of the class, two other women asked my paralegal for her card!

My associate attorney, Lori, had a similar experience when she accidentally dropped her business cards out of her wallet while on the checkout line at Target. The man in line behind her bent down to pick them up and noticed that she was as attorney at a family law firm. He wasn't involved in a domestic dispute. He was a financial professional who specialized as a trial expert in divorces. He had recently had a heart attack due to "occupational stress," and had heard about this "new collaborative method" that was supposed to be less stressful for the spouses *and* for the professionals.

He asked Lori about her card (of course, it says that she is a collaborative attorney), and she explained that she worked for a family law firm that focuses on out-of-court divorce resolutions. Once they had both paid for their items, they sat down at the coffee shop at the front of the store, specifically so that Lori could answer his questions. Lori explained the collaborative process and that it would mean that the professional would no longer be subjected to an opposing counsel's stressful cross examinations while on the stand in front of the judge. He attended the very next collaborative training, and when one of his clients needed a divorce attorney, he recommended our firm.

Even my IT guy, Bill, understands the collaborative process and pitches it whenever possible. He attended a Star Trek convention, and when a Vulcan friend mentioned that his daughter wasn't sure if her baby's father was a Romulan or a Klingon, Bill explained that the collaborative process would work for a paternity case. We like to say that the collaborative divorce process should be the final frontier for domestic disputes!

Ensure that your support staff is experienced with their versions of your pitch. Just because they are not lawyers doesn't mean they can't market your firm as well as you can.

Do You Charge Enough? (Pitching Too Low)

Most likely, if you are a solo or small firm lawyer, you do not. There is an appropriate time for *pro bono*, low bono, reduced rate, modest means, or other special programs. But for regular clients who do not fit into the strict requirements of these models, are you charging as much as other attorneys in your community with similar experience as yours? If not, why not?

Often when people are under charging, it is because they don't have the confidence to request more. But the worst that can happen is that the potential client will say "no." And usually they won't just say "no," but they may counter with a lower rate, a rate that may still be acceptable to you and that probably is higher than what you are currently charging if you are undercutting yourself.

Don't bid against yourself. By not charging as much as the "movers and shakers" in your community, you may ensure that you are never viewed as one of them, not only by potential clients, but also by colleagues (the ones getting the big cases). You may inadvertently develop a reputation as a "budget" lawyer. Or potential clients may feel that, because of your low rate, they are paying you to get experience when they'd rather pay more for someone who offers expertise. People associate expertise with price, and, by charging what you're worth, you will be viewed as more of an expert.

Don't sell yourself short. Think of the special qualities that you have to offer that make you an exceptional lawyer. Whatever it is, can you quantify how much this special expertise is worth?

Of course, you don't want to price yourself out of the market because what good is it to charge $500 per hour if you can't get any cases? Before increasing your rate, research common rates in your community of those at your experience level. But also remember that you may have much more to offer because of your unique skills, because of where you went to school, because your first career was in a field that adds value to your pedigree, or for some other reason.

And there are always ways to increase your worth. Publish a book. (See more on publishing at page 63, et. seq.) Present often. (See more on presenting at page 93, et. seq.) Become known as an expert in your field, and you will soon be able to charge the higher fees associated with experts and big firm lawyers.

Remember that it is harder to ask for more money than to agree to less money. If you quote a potential client a $300 hourly rate, it will be difficult to later request that they pay $400 per hour for the same services. But if you quote $400 per hour, they may agree to that amount, or they may counter for a bit lower. If you agree to that lower amount, they will be pleased because they will feel that they are getting a good deal, even though they may be paying more than what you expected to receive. Consider that, by setting the anchor at a high price, you set the anchor in the potential client's mind at that high price, and you negotiate from there. But if you allow your potential client to begin the negotiation, you will likely be starting at a much lower number, making it more difficult to work yourself up to the higher amount that you are worth.

Consider publishing your rates so that you don't waste time with potential clients who will never be able to afford your services.

When considering whether to increase your rates, set a trial period during which you request a higher rate. Document the percentage of cases that you sign at that hourly rate, the percentage who do not retain you at all, and the percentage who ask for a reduced rate. Compare this to your prior records of the percentage of folks who retained you at your lower hourly rate to determine whether the increase has proved more lucrative.

And always remember not to sell yourself short. You are as valuable as you think you are!

Publish

Introduction to Publishing Fortes

Why publish? Because it gives you credibility and it turns you into an expert in your field. When you read books, don't you assume that the authors are experts on the subject about which they are writing? And this assumption is generally correct because, during the writing process, you become much more knowledgeable about your subject.

But, you object, you are a lawyer, not a writer. Where do you even begin? In this section, you'll learn the Who, What, When, Where, Why, and How of publishing. I'll provide you with helpful tips, as well as errors to avoid. We'll not only discuss book writing, but also smaller scale publishing, like blogging and writing for journals.

While producing a book may seem like a daunting task, there is no time like the present. Once you have read this section, I strongly encourage you to get started on your book. I have mentored any number of folks to finally get their books out there, and, while intimidating, once you start, the book will seem to write itself. If you need a book mentor, consider reaching out to me at Joryn@OpenPalmPress.com; I'll be happy to help.

And, before you know it, you'll be the author of your own book!

PUBLISHING BASICS

Publishing frequently on a subject creates credibility for the author. Credibility is the ability to write clear and compelling blogs, articles, tweets, and books that people will read, relate to, and share with others.

Writing helps you learn and understand your subject better, which again leads to credibility because you will come across as more knowledgeable when you discuss your subject.

Who is your reader? First, construct an avatar of your perfect reader or picture a real person whom you want your words to reach. What does she want to know? Identify the burning questions this reader wants answered.

What do you offer that's unique? Every piece you write should offer your distinctive take on a particular subject. There's no point in being a clone of an existing legal personality. No one has yet written your book. Your perspective is yours alone.

What's the specific next step you want your reader to take right after she puts down your book or finishes reading your article? Think of your writing as an extended version of your pitch. As such, it is critical to include a call to action in every piece you write, just as you do when you pitch in person out loud.

Where do you publish? It is important that you publish in a place where your ideal reader, your avatar client, will find you.

How often do you publish? You should publish as often and as consistently as possible, while still offering fresh, quality content. You don't have to post every day, but you should post at least a couple of times each week. Keep track of how many readers and comments you get based on the day and time you post.

Set aside a specific hour each day to write. If possible, avoid using a writing service. If you must, be sure that it is not a ghostwriter situation with someone who knows nothing about practicing law or how to offer the services you provide. Instead, it should be a true collaboration.

Make sure that your article is well written regarding grammar, syntax, spelling, etc. Even if you are making stellar points, if they are hiding behind poor grammar, it will be difficult for you to find a publisher. Publishers are offered many articles, so you must make it as easy on them as possible to publish yours. Have a friend or colleague proofread your article before you submit it. At the very least, pick your best-read staffer and ask him or her to have a quick read. Your staff person will learn something and you can ensure that there are no glaring typos.

Be choosy when determining which journal to send your article to. It is unethical (in the publishing world) to submit your publication to more than one journal at a time. But to avoid wasting time, don't just submit your article to the most prestigious journal if you really don't feel that it could be published there. Don't sell yourself short, but be realistic so that you don't waste time. Besides, the most prestigious journal may not be the one that reaches your target audience.

Don't be offended if you are asked to revise your article and resubmit it. Instead, be happy; you weren't rejected!

What types of written work do you publish?

- Academic papers relevant to your mission;
- Blogs;
- Articles;
- Chapters;
- Books;
- White papers;
- Newsletters; and
- Comments and posts in LinkedIn, Facebook, etc. discussion groups.

Where do you find your material?

- Record your presentations (more on presenting later) and the Q&A after. Then post the video on YouTube and on your website. Transcribe it and then give away the e-book as a "free gift" to potential clients on your website;
- Audience questions can be the kernel that pops into a written piece;
- Top tips;
- Worst mistakes;
- Best strategies;
- Commentaries on news that is relevant to your practice; and
- Stories from your own life, or your own practice.

How often might you be featured in the media?

- On your own TV show;
- On your own radio show;
- On YouTube or Google Hangout;
- With your own newspaper article;
- With your magazine or e-zine article;
- On your own website;
- On your own podcast;
- As a guest on someone else's podcast;

- As a guest on a talk radio show;
- As a guest on TV;
- As quoted in someone else's magazine article; or
- As a guest blogger on someone else's website.

PUBLISHING TIPS

- Imagine the avatar of your perfect reader. This may be the same avatar as your perfect client, or it might be someone else, like a referral source or a partner who serves the same clients as you do but with a different or complementary service.
- Identify the big, burning question that your avatar wants answered.
- Offer a unique perspective. Write about something in your practice area that bothers you. Take a stand, and become known for what you stand for.
- Always include the specific next step that you want your reader to take right after they finish reading. As always, that call to action is crucial.
- Publish in the appropriate journals. Be sure to appeal to the journal's scope and aim. Always follow the journal's rules and procedures.
- Get featured as a contributor in a relevant magazine.
- Post regularly and consistently.
- Create a weekly editorial calendar; plan your blog schedule.
- When blogging, use key words to increase search engine optimization.
- Always employ good grammar, syntax, and spelling.
- Be choosy, but realistic when submitting articles to journals for publication.
- Take positive criticism well and apply it.
- Write a white paper (an authoritative report giving information or proposals on an issue) on the future of your practice area. Carry professionally designed and printed copies with you, and hand them out when appropriate. Also, post it on-line, on your website or as a guest author on someone else's website.
- Record detailed information about a project on which you are working, and after a month has passed, or significant progress has been made, prepare a report showing the progress made and your impact, as well as any testimonials you've received about it.
- Document cases you've worked, including interviews of those involved. Save this material for use later, even if it's too fresh to write about in the moment.
- Create your book map (an outline of the entire book) early, but revise it often as your experiences impact the content of your book.
- Create a map for each chapter.
- Understand that no one has already written the book you will write, the

book by *you*. Write your book. Aim for 35,000 words.

- Organize your blogs and articles into the map of your book; expand any that require additional discussion to fit as chapters into your book, 3000 (1000-5000) words for each chapter.
- In fact, review your writings of any kind over the last year, including letters to clients, letters to counsel, pleadings, documents, handouts, etc., to determine whether they might dually function as chapters in your book.
- Decide whether to publish conventionally (traditional publishing), publish cooperatively (hybrid publishing), or self-publish.[2]
- Find an editor whom you can trust, someone who understands who you are and who complements your existing writing abilities, and who comes recommended by other writers.
- When designing your cover, start with fiverr.com.
- Request a foreword. Start with the perfect person for the book you've written, even if he's a celebrity or at the top of his practice area. If you don't ask, he can't say "yes."
- When you request the foreword, send him a presentable draft of the book, as well as a suggested draft of his foreword.
- Request testimonials. Same rules for testimonials as for forewords. Or you can interview your clients for testimonials. See *Asking for Testimonials*, at page 131.
- Publish your book. There's no time like the present, so start writing!
- If you feel like it's too big a job to do, reach out to another author who's willing to mentor you in the writing of your book.[3]

PUBLISHING ERRORS

- Failing to write to your avatar;
- Offering stale material;
- Failing to let your avatar know how you want him to proceed;
- Failing to abide by a journal's rules and procedures;
- Posting less that once a week;
- Using poor grammar, syntax, and spelling;
- Forgetting your call to action;
- Simply submitting your article to the most prestigious journal without considering which journals your ideal reader reads most often;
- Taking criticism poorly;
- Failing to ask the best people for your foreword or for your testimonials; and
- Giving up before reaching out to an author-mentor.

---

[2] Contact *Open Palm Press* (Joryn@OpenPalmPress.com) for details on hybrid publishing.

[3] Consider reaching out to me, as I have mentored numerous would-be authors. Joryn@OpenPalmPress.com.

PUBLISH

Do you have authority in your practice area or in the law? Are you perceived by the public as "the expert," as having the right answers to their questions? Credibility enables you to write clear and compelling blogs, articles, tweets, and books that people will read, relate to, and share with others.

First, determine who your reader is. That should not be difficult at this point. Remember your perfect listener from constructing your pitch? The avatar to whom you spoke when you crafted your pitch? This is the same person, the perfect reader whom you want your words to reach, but in writing now. What does she want to know? Identify the burning questions your avatar, this reader wants answered.

What can you offer this reader that is unique? Every piece you write should offer your unique perspective. No one has yet written *your* blog, *your* article, or *your* book.

Creating a blog is not hard. Go on-line, search "how to write a blog" and follow the instructions. I won't waste your time now explaining the steps here.

It is the writing itself that challenges many of us. But ideas themselves are not that tough to come by. It's just that being able to identify topics about which to write is a talent that most people have not tried to stimulate or to enhance. Once you've developed the aptitude, however, it becomes second nature.

What happened today in a case that stole your breath away? What happened that scared the crud out of you? When you pitched him, what tale did your listener share in response? What difficulty did your colleague share with you at lunch, seeking your input and advice? These are all fertile and abundant topics about which you should at least be blogging.

You will often find that one topic leads to the next. Sometimes, comments on your blog will suggest related productive topics for you to discuss, about which to write. If you suggested the right way to correct the problem, perhaps comments people left for you to that piece suggested other corrections about which you can then blog.

Be yourself when you blog. People will want to relate to you. What differentiates bloggers from the old news reporters is their use of voice. Although the information that you provide will be why they *begin* to read, it is your personality that will *keep* them reading. As scary as it may seem to you, your readers want to feel that they know you.

Think about the posts that attract you. Don't you feel that you know their authors? I know that I do.

Always place links both to highly trafficked websites and to your prior posts within your subsequent posts. This will increase the number of people who click over to check you out, and it will also boost your blog's SEO.

So will including photos, by the way. While readers come to your blog for content and/or because they like you personally, let there be no doubt that they are attracted to visual images. And while you can always use free, on-line images, it's just as easy and certainly more effective if you take your cell phone out and snap two images each that work for every blog you post.

Respond to comments that others leave on your blog. This is your opportunity to connect directly with your readers. At the very least, on-line protocol finds it perfectly acceptable to say "thank you for your comment."

In fact, part of my *Profile* advice later in this volume is that you should read blogs written by others and leave comments for the writers whom you like. Sign up for LinkedIn and Facebook discussion groups that make sense for your practice area and your preferences. As a side effect, you can participate in on-line discussions and find topics worthy of writing about that way.

And this is how you can also use social media to boost your own blog. Post your newest blog to the discussion groups to which relates. This will make it easier for potential readers to find your blog in the first place.

Now what about re-purposing content you've already posted? A blog is generally around 500 words, give or take 200. (Although I personally violate that rule all the time. And some SEO pundits now advise that 2000-word blogs will capitalize your on-line profile.) But a 500-word blog can easily be turned into a 2000-word article, or, better still, a 1000-to-5000-word chapter in your soon-to-be-book.

For those of you who blog regularly, have you published your book yet? If not, then sit down and list all of the blogs you've ever written. Organize them by topic. Is there a unifying theme among a majority of them? Now that some time has passed since you wrote many of them, how many can be improved and expanded into book chapters?

Once you've organized those that naturally group together into a structured symphony unified by a common theme, what holes do you see that need to be filled? Perhaps you're too close to see it; ask a friend to review it with you to help you identify the gaps. Now you've got some more blogging to do, don't you?

What's the specific next step you want your reader to take right after she puts down your article or finishes reading your blog? Don't forget to include a call to action in every piece you write.

Finally, title your blog. Obviously, as you've written it, you've played with some potential titles as you went along. Once you've reached your conclusion, though, you already have a good idea of what you want to call it. The trick is to come up with a title that is search engine friendly but still accurate; you want people to click for it, but not to be disappointed when they actually start reading it.

Increasing your SEO involves using those magic "keywords" that everyone talks about. There are some great posts on Hubspot, among others, that will help you find and apply keywords to your titles and your content to increase your SEO and your (on-line) visibility.

But now we're moving into *Profile*, which I will cover later in this volume. Suffice it to say that you can search for "writing blog titles" and you'll find everything you ever wanted to know about the subject, many times in easy-to-follow instructions.

Establish your credibility, your authority in your practice area, easily, by publishing.

Find the Right Publications

Finding the right publications in which to publish your articles is as important as the content of what you publish. You could write the most well-thought, entertaining, and informative article on the practice of law, but if you publish it in the *Journal of Neurosurgery*, you won't have many readers, and those who do read it probably won't have much interest in it because they are not your target audience. Thus, it is crucial to understand who your target audience is. What journals might this audience read? For that matter, what journals do *you* read?

When contemplating where to publish, consider the type of article you would like to publish. Are there limitations or length requirements in the journals in which you are considering publishing? Have you complied with the journal's preferred house style? You should be able to find it on the journal's website.

What is the journal's scope and aim? Does your article meet those? You can usually find them on the journal's homepage. Look for a section titled "About the Journal," "Full Aims and Scope," or something similar. Browsing this page will provide you with important information about whether your research might be a good match for the journal.

Does the journal give advice to potential authors? Have you followed that advice? Do you need an invitation from the journal to submit your article? If so, how do you obtain one?

Look at the references you cite in your article. Where were those articles published? Read articles in journals that interest you and that directly relate to your own research. Search with keywords of your manuscript to determine if the journal has published work similar to yours. If you find three to five articles published within the last five years that are similar to yours, you're on the right track. If you find articles directly related to your own research, then that is the appropriate journal to which you should consider submitting your own article. Cite related articles and compare your results with the results of others.

I can't say too often that you must ensure that your article is well written regarding grammar, syntax, spelling, etc. Even if you are making stellar points, if they are hiding behind poor grammar, it will be difficult to find a publisher. Have a friend or colleague proofread your article before you submit it.

There are various resources available to help you choose a publisher. *The Springer Journal Selector* uses semantic technology, and can help you determine appropriate journals. *JournalGuide* is a free tool that helps researchers evaluate and compare scholarly journals.

It is unethical in publishing circles to submit your publication to more than one journal at a time, so be choosy when considering where to send your article. Make sure that you have not missed important deadlines. And keep at it. Just because one journal rejects your submission does not mean that all journals will.

Additionally, don't just submit your article to the most prestigious journal with the highest impact factor. Instead, objectively evaluate whether your manuscript is suitable for such a publication, or you'll waste valuable time and effort revising and resubmitting. Consider how accessible that journal will actually be to your target audience. It doesn't matter how prominent the journal is if no one is actually reading your article. Then again, if you aim high initially, even if you are denied, you can always use the feedback to improve your article for another journal.

Don't be offended if you are asked to revise your article and resubmit it. You didn't get rejected! The publisher felt that you had something valuable to say but that it just needed a bit more work. When you do resubmit the revised article, include a detailed cover letter that explains the changes that you made, and, if appropriate, why you didn't make certain requested changes. And, of course, always be polite when dealing with publishers.

If you are having difficulty finding a publisher, you may want to revise your article so that it is more tailored to the themes that the journal publishes.

Where you publish will influence the exposure of your work, how often it is cited, its ultimate impact, and your credibility.

Once you've become proficient at blogging and tweeting and writing articles, it is now time to write your book. Let's cover that next.

Write Your Book

We'll start this discussion at the beginning of your finished manuscript, although you won't commence your writing here. You'll actually initiate your writing with the meat of your book, after you map it out, and worry about the details of the final publication later. But for now, let's lay bare some of the mysterious secrets of manuscript writing. We'll uncover how each segment of your book is generated, starting with the opening pages.

Dedication

Each book should commence with a dedication. Make it short and concise. Consider why you are writing your book and how you might advance your mission. Here are a couple examples:

- I'd like to thank Mr. Trundle, my eighth-grade English teacher, for always being there for me when I was first learning to write creatively.
- I want to dedicate this book to my husband. Tom, thanks for being so supportive and for standing by me all these years.

Testimonials

For the section on *What Others Are Saying About This Book*, should you decide to include it, ask clients. Ask respected colleagues. And ask celebrities. You might want to send out as many as 30 requests, especially to the celebrities on your list. Clients and professionals will be flattered; I have a 90% success rate on those requests. Celebrities are more difficult, of course. You'll have a much higher success rate if you choose a) celebrities with whom you share a connection, and b) celebrities who are actively promoting their profiles on-line. The latter are just as easy to reach as the former; they have posted their contact information on the Internet. You may end up negotiating with their assistants, but so much the better. You'll get faster results. I certainly did!

Send your requests with sample testimonials upon which the writers may model their own. I've included sample requests in Appendix 10.

A testimonial for your book should not be about how great its author (you) is; it should be about the content of the book. This is a good example:

> This book contains the most revolutionary and innovative thinking I've heard in ten years. If you are involved in a criminal, civil, or domestic dispute, you must read this book to understand the enormity of the choice of process you have to make.

Consumer testimonials should be from people who are in your target audience, your clients. Expert testimonials should be from people who are at the top of your field. Obviously, the testimonials themselves should be tailored accordingly.

Which celebrities you ask will depend on your contacts and on your preferences. Will you approach those to whom you are somehow connected and to whom you can get some kind of introduction? What about those who have an interest in the focus of your book? How about those who are active in the media and who therefore have the public trust? These are possible choices; you may be able to think of more.

If you decide to approach celebrities to whom you have no connection, or if you have no choice, then take a shotgun approach to 30 or so stars. Who are their managers or their booking agents? Who are their management companies? You may want to pay someone to research that information and to obtain contact e-mails and phone numbers for all 30 celebrities' booking agents.

Once you identify from whom to request a testimonial, send a PDF of your book that is password protected: save it so that editing is not allowed. They should be able only to print and read and hand scribe on their hard copies, if they feel it necessary.

When they agree, pin them to dates. Identify how you will get the feedback. Will you talk by phone? Will they return marked-up copies? Then make their jobs easy; write three testimonials for each them (you don't want them all picking the exact same testimonial) and let them choose the ones they prefer and make any changes that they feel are necessary to make them their own.

Once they come in, choose the best three or four (for content and author identity) for the back of your book and include the rest inside it, in *What Others Are Saying About This Book.*

Don't be afraid to re-write any testimonial that is not well enough written; don't be afraid to cut extraneous comments from those you want for the back of your book. (Your space there will be limited. You can include the entire testimonial inside, if you like.) Just remember to run any changes and anything you've rewritten by their authors before publishing them.

FOREWORD

The next component of your book will be the foreword. As an author, you should consider who would be the right person to write the foreword for your manuscript. Again, consider your mission. The secret here is to find the most famous or well-respected person you can who can support the vision for your book. If it's a book about law, then the top person in that practice area may be the ideal person to write the foreword for it. Consider whether to seek a person who enjoys a profile of national significance, or whether to ask someone with an international reputation.

Of course, you may want to consider asking an appropriate celebrity to write that foreword instead. I've done both.

Keep in mind that, among other things and like your testimonials, your foreword is a marketing tool. The person who writes it will inevitably market the book to his contacts and followers. You will use his name to market the book to your perfect readers. Make sure that you provide him with at least one clean copy when it is published, along with your gracious and effusive thank-you note.

Prepare a professionally written synopsis of your manuscript to include in your request that he consider writing your foreword. (You'll use this later to describe your book on the back cover and on Amazon.) It should appeal to his own goals and interests, which, if you've chosen wisely, should coordinate with your own. It should call out to him to write the foreword to this book, because it will add to his own credibility or champion a cause about which he cares.

Always send a pre-publication copy of your manuscript to the person you've asked to write your foreword or to give you a testimonial. He should want to read your book before giving you that testimonial, or writing that foreword! If you're concerned about protecting its contents, then save it as a PDF that can't be edited and send that. And don't send a rough draft of anything! You don't want this person whom you respect highly enough to request that he write your foreword to think that you've written an unprofessional or sloppy book.

If the person you've targeted responds that he would do it but is too busy, then write the foreword for him and offer it to him already written. (Be careful to research his background to ensure that you include all of the reasons why the public should admire him and respect his opinion. If he later removes these details, you may have to explain that the foreword is all about him, not about you. This happened to me. Luckily, my writer understood right away and reincorporated those details.) This way, you aren't asking him to take the time to actually write it. If he agrees to put his name on what you've already written, all he has to do is give you the "okay." But it's more likely that he'll then personalize it, adding those final details that you couldn't possibly have known, despite your research into his background.

Don't panic if you don't have anything worth sending him just yet. If you've stroked your target properly, he'll wait. It's perfectly acceptable to tell him that you'll send him something in a week or two. I actually kept someone waiting for two months before I was able to send the book to him. (He was very patient. Thank you, Ron Ousky!)

I've included a chapter here on how to write a foreword. See *Write Your Foreword,* at page 79.

The next question, of course, is "How do I ask?" Some advisors recommend against sending an e-mail. They'll suggest that you create a short video and send it in a direct tweet to the people you target. In it, you should:

- State your name and what you do.
- Be complimentary of how that person has made you better at whatever it

is that you do. Thank him for that.

- Respectfully request that he do you the honor of writing the foreword to your book, a book that, without his influence, you would never have written.
- Thank him for considering your request.

The video should take anywhere from 15 to 30 seconds. For the foreword, send it to the top three to five people in your practice area. But send it to only one person at a time; after all, what would you do if more than one says "yes"?

But I disagree. I have found e-mails and snail mail (depending on the person to whom I'm sending the request) to be perfectly acceptable and efficacious, as well as more efficient for me, personally. See my sample foreword request in Appendix 9.

INTRODUCTION

Now comes your introduction. This is your opportunity to introduce your reader to your passion. Communicate why you have dedicated the time and energy to writing your book. It's all about the emotion behind and the heart you put into what you do. It's a marketing piece about you as a person, but also about your vision and your mission. Your introduction should encourage your reader to feel that you are a credible and influential person, honest and trustworthy, and that your mission is truly worthy.

Explain to your reader why you love what you do. Enlighten him as to your drive to do what you do. If you don't love what you do, then it will look as though you do it strictly for the money. Not terribly endearing.

Explain why you are qualified to do what you do. However, although you must explain (notice I didn't say "brag" or "boast" about) your credentials, you must also be humble. (This is a difficult but critical line to draw. If you have difficulty with this, your editor may be able to help you.)

You will mention the type of people you help and how what you do professionally helps them. Identify particular clients, if not (with permission) by name, then by a description of their circumstances and how you helped them. Just be careful how you go about describing your clients because they are also probably your readers, and you don't want to accidentally insult them. Also, remember that you'll be seeking testimonials from them.

Conclude your introduction with your goal for the manuscript. Apprise your readers of your objective and enable them to buy into it. You will conclude your book with a call to action, so set the stage for that now.

Your introduction may be the only thing that someone peruses before deciding whether to buy your book. So, if that someone picks up your book or takes a quick look on Amazon and reads your intro, you want her to deduce that you are an authority, a reputable, credible person who has the credentials for writing your book, so that she is interested in listening to what you have to say.

CONTENT

Next, let's talk about the actual substance of this manuscript. Most authors of business books start by developing a chapter map; they map out the entire book before they even commence the writing process. (Well, of course, you've already written all those blog posts that are becoming or will become chapters. For now, you'll just include those in your map.) Ideally, you should have, not only the topics of each chapter defined, but also the subchapters to help you focus the content of each chapter and to prevent you from repeating yourself. This map will later become your table of contents, and you may well decide not to include the subchapters. But they will be useful in the writing process.

There are many shortcuts to content creation. Repurposing your earlier written work of any kind is the most valuable. As I've mentioned already, collect and organize all of your prior writings. This includes blogs, articles, letters to clients, motions, briefs, summaries of interviews, e-mails, forms, and anything else that you (or anyone on your staff, for that matter) may have written that is or may be pertinent to the topics covered in your book. Discard anything that simply does not mesh.

There are several other quick avenues to content creation to which I subscribe:

- For those of us who present well, especially if you are not as comfortable with the writing process, record your presentations and the Q&A after.
  - ✓ Once you do, not only do you now have the raw material to create at least one video to post on YouTube and on your website (thereby bolstering your profile), but you can also send the audio to a transcription service. (Try www.fiverr.com; I've obtained wonderful product from them very inexpensively and the site is certainly user-friendly.)
  - ✓ You can then (with a little help from an editor) turn the transcript into an e-book, and into at least one chapter in your physical book, depending on its length.
  - ✓ In addition, questions from the audience and discussion with participants can serve to seed additional written chapters.
- Ask Google to notify you of anything having to do with the topic that interests you. You will thus be apprised of anything in the news that relates to your subject matter, and you can explore that issue while it is current. If you blog about it, you ensure its timeliness; but you can still include an extended discussion of it in your book.
- Stories from your own life and your own practice can serve as grist for your mill. Many experts advise against sharing your personal stories; I disagree. People respond to personal stories. Sensitize yourself to the issues that you take for granted; they may help you to connect the dots for your readers.

I find writing fairly easy, but that wasn't always the case. Initially, I had a difficult time and it was a slow slog through a muddy bog every time I took pen to paper. But, one day, I was driving home and I had a great idea for a chapter. I was afraid I would lose it before I could get back in front of a computer, so I picked up my cell phone (while I was stopped at a red light) and I started an e-mail to myself to record the idea. Then I hit the microphone button on the keypad. When I started to tell myself the idea I had had, the phone was transcribing everything I had to say. It was too easy! I ended up actually dictating the draft of an entire chapter.

I converse at approximately 190 words per minute. I soon discovered that, with pauses to think through the next paragraph, I could dictate 1000 words in my 12-minute drive home, assuming that I had a good idea of what I wanted the chapter to cover.

So, of course, I recommend this method of writing your book. But you may find your own technique. (If you do, please don't hesitate to share it with me.)

In today's market, your chapters should be 2,000 – 3,500 words long. (Although this one is longer, you'll notice it has subparts). You may be as brief as 1,000 words. If it's a compelling human-interest story, it may be as long as 5,000 words. On the other hand, don't shortchange your reader by cutting your story short in order to abide by a pre-conceived word count. In the end, a good editor can always help you shorten an overly long story if it is truly that, overly long.

A good business book can range between 35,000 words and 70,000 words, depending on the style and the content. My first was two books because I had written too much, in my opinion, for one book. So, my first book, *War or Peace*, was 54,330 words, including the testimonials, the foreword, the table of contents, and the title page, all of the required but not substantial parts of the manuscript. It was also 168 pages (of substance) long, in a 6" x 9" format, a standard layout for a business book.

My second, *I Never Saw My Father Again*, was 63,219 words long, again, including what I think of as non-essentials. It was 220 pages, also in a 6" x 9" format.

Thus far, we've only discussed the practical details of book writing. But there are many aspects to writing your manuscript that are intangible, if you will. Every book, for example, should both evince emotion and evoke that emotion in its readers. The words you choose can help you manifest those feelings. Identify the sentiments that you'd like your readers to feel, and then ascertain all of the synonyms for that word that you are able and use them throughout your writing, as appropriate.

If you are writing a motivational book, for example, pepper your manuscript with words and phrases like: motivation, exhilarating, gets my heart pumping, life-changing, dare, inspiration, drive, challenge yourself, enthusiasm, spur, stimulate, dream big, etc.

The words you elect to use will stimulate your readers to feel what you want them to feel. So, write in the words that either define the emotion or are the physical manifestations of that emotion, in order for the reader to feel it.

Most books should have an emotion for every chapter. Business books are not exempt from this. Through the intentional choice of our words, we can inspire the reader to feel like students, in need of help, motivated, etc.

We don't want to write the types of books that people start but don't finish. So, let's give your reader reasons to keep reading. For example, in chapter two, we can say, ". . . but I will get into this in more detail in chapter six so that you don't ever make that type of mistake and lose out on potential clients."

Use hooks. Most people know that a hook in the intro and to start a book is good, but go a step further and use several more hooks as the reader progresses. Not many, but a few. After chapter six or seven, you may only need one more hook. If the reader has gotten that far, she is intent on reading the rest of it.

Every business book needs a call to action. Discuss this with your reader at your earliest opportunity. Perhaps it's to go to your website, contact you via e-mail, or to pass the book along. Whatever it is, express it powerfully.

The best emotions with which to leave your reader are determination, awe, motivation, respect for your knowledge, and desire for your services.

I personally don't think an epilogue is needed in a non-fiction book. However, it's a good place to sum up the gist of the book in approximately 2,000 words. It's also a good place for your ultimate call to action. (You should have these sprinkled throughout the book.)

ACKNOWLEDGEMENTS

The acknowledgements section is where the author thanks those to whom he feels grateful for helping him to make the book possible. Some people put this early in the book; others close with it.

ABOUT THE AUTHOR

You should also include an *About the Author* section, in which you describe who you are, and what makes you credible, relatable, and interesting. What are your credentials, your background, your qualities, and your hobbies? What about your family?

You will also want to list any sources you used to write the book. If you cited statistics, quotes, or other authors to lend credibility to what you have said, include that information here, at the end, after the substance.

RECOMMENDED READING

Finally, you might want to include a section of *Recommended Reading*. You can reach out to authors whose books have helped you, thank them for their expertise, and apprise them that you have recommended their book in your own. This is another marketing tool. It is likely, when your book is published, that those authors, like the author of your foreword, will promote it to their circles of influence.

They might also write great reviews for your book if you send them copies and request that they consider doing that.

Notice that I have included my own recommended reading list for you in Appendix 8.

TITLE

You never get a second chance to make a good first impression, and that holds true for the title of your book. It is a potential reader's first glimpse into your book. Be original and creative. Consider using literary devices like puns, rhymes, or alliteration to give your title a pleasing sound. Tell the reader what the book is about, and, while short titles are recommended, don't shy away from long titles and subtitles if you can't tell him without a longer title or, preferably, subtitle.

Consider an important object, character, or idea from your book, and start brainstorming. Once you've brainstormed at least three titles, have those you trust rate them to determine which is their favorite choice, and why. Ask them for other ideas, as well.

I like to send out an e-mail to my trusted advisors when it comes to titles (as well as covers). This small group survey (usually no more than 100 people with an interest in the topic of the book) gives me sufficient feedback to make an informed decision.

FRONT COVER

We shouldn't judge a book by its cover, but when it comes to actual books, we do. A sloppy, boring, low quality, or unprofessional design can result in negligible interest in your book. If you're not in the position yet to hire a professional cover designer, you can still design a professional looking cover if you follow these tips.

As you are writing your book, be on the lookout for colors, fonts, images, and patterns that resonate with the theme of your book. Look at the covers of books similar to yours to determine what you like and don't like. Just as you brainstorm ideas for your book, compile these so that when you are ready to design your cover, you have a good idea of what you want it to look like, rather than facing an intimidating blank canvas.

Like your title, your book cover should set the right tone for your book. If it is a serious book, use muted or neutral colors and sharp or blocky font. If it covers a more lighthearted subject, use brighter colors, cartoon images, and loopy lettering.

If you are using an image, it should tell a story and give insight as to the subject of the book. You also want to make sure that you use quality images, like those from www.istockphoto.com. Use software like Picasa, Apple Photos, or Fotor to edit your images so that you don't destroy their quality. Images for book covers should be at least 1,700 pixels wide, but an image that wraps around the entire cover should be even larger. You can always reduce size and quality, but increasing size is impossible without decreasing quality.

Finally, keep it simple. Ensure that your title and name are large enough to get the attention that they deserve.

Proofread your cover. There's no easier way to lose readers than with sloppy grammar and spelling errors on it. (Authors often include a star with the author of the foreword's name in it on the front cover. Don't make the same mistake I did; I was so excited to publish my first book that I missed the cover artist's misspelling of the word "foreword.")

BACK COVER

What goes on the back of your book? This is where you, again, use the professional description of your book, extolling its virtues and explaining why anyone picking it up should read it. (This will also go on Amazon in the description section.) This is also where you put the three or four best testimonials, along with the givers' credentials. Here is where you share that you have new insights or a new approach to the subject matter.

It's always fun to include four or five questions on the back that invite the peruser to "Turn to page ***" to find the answer to the query. Ensure that the page to which they turn is perceptive and intriguing, a page-turner. If you keep them inside the book for any length of time, they may well buy it.

ISBN

Your book will not be available for bookstores, libraries, or just about anywhere else without an ISBN number. If you want your book in multiple places – e-book, Amazon, and Barnes and Noble – you'll need more than one ISBN number.

Bowker.com is the only place to get ISBN numbers. You can buy one ISBN for $125, but it is far more cost-effective to pay for the next smallest package, ten ISBN numbers for $250. (You need a separate ISBN for each version of the book you publish, so your hard copy will be assigned a different ISBN than your e-version.) They can take up to three weeks to actually get to you so keep that in mind, as well. Here's the link where you can obtain them: https://www.myidentifiers.com/get-your-isbn-now.

COPYRIGHT

Copyrighting your book is important because it prevents others from simply copying your book and then selling it without your permission. Registering your copyright gives others notice of your claim to the copyright. Registration creates constructive notice, which allows you to assert your copyright against anyone from the date of registration forward, regardless of whether they had prior knowledge of your book.

Registering your copyright is relatively easy and inexpensive, especially considering the intellectual property protection that it provides to you. Go to copyright.gov to register your book. There is an on-line portal to register copyrights for written works. Simply complete the form and pay the fee, and your copyright will be registered.

FORMAT

When submitting your book to a publisher, find out what format they recommend, and follow it. Avoid using fancy fonts, oddly sized font, colors, unusual margins, and strange illustrations. Adapt your manuscript based on each publisher's requirements, although they should be fairly similar. The following are generally accepted guidelines for manuscripts, but these may change somewhat based on the size you ultimately choose for your book:

- Font should be black, 12-point, Times New Roman, Cambria, or Courier New.
- Margins should be one-inch on all four sides.

- Indentations should be a half-inch for the first line of each paragraph.
- Double space the document.
- Align the document to the left.
- Begin numbering pages when the substance begins, not on the title page.
- Include your last name, your title, and the page number in the page header of every page except for the title page. Align the header to the right, and do not include it on your title page.
- Begin chapters on new pages, preferably on the right side of the book. Center the chapter title about a third down the page. Skip a couple of spaces, and begin the text of the chapter.
- Use italics to stress words, rather than underlining or bold.
- Use a single character space only, not two spaces, between sentences.
- On your title page, include the following:
  - ✓ Your contact information, aligned left and single spaced, near the top;
  - ✓ Include your word count at the top of the right side of the title page;
  - ✓ Approximately halfway down the page, centered, enter the full manuscript title in all caps or mixed caps;
  - ✓ Double-space down, then type "by" or "a novel by" or "a story by"; and
  - ✓ On the next double-spaced line, add your name.

PUBLISH

Obviously, this is an abbreviated rendition of everything that the would-be author should consider when setting out to birth a book. But appreciate that you, too, can write a book. For many, many years, my mother swore up and down that I would write a book. My consistent rejoinder was "I don't have a book in me." Little did I know how easy it is to produce a book. Or, at least, how not-as-hard-as-I-thought-it-would-be it is. I've now written, counting this one, five books in just two-and-a-half years. When you have something to say, and you've discovered the habit of recording your thoughts and opinions in writing, it becomes easy to write a book.

And, as the old joke goes, "How do you eat an elephant?"

"One bite at a time."

Generally speaking, there are three types of publishers; traditional, hybrid, and self. A trade publishing house will pick up few authors, and, even then, most books lose money rather than making it. Hybrid publishers' services fall somewhere between self-publishing and a traditional publisher. Hybrid publishers differ greatly in their terms, but they generally offer authors some level of in-house editorial expertise and distribution support, in exchange for a fee and a share in the profits from sales. As for self-publishing, these days it's a breeze.

If you are reading this, you're not publishing a book to make money from it anyway; you're publishing to accomplish your mission, and your book will both add to your credibility and provide you with an impressive business card. So, my advice is to self-publish, or to go with a small hybrid publishing house like *Open Palm Press.*

WRITE YOUR FOREWORD

A foreword (not a "forward" or a "foreward") comes "before the word"; it is a short introduction to a book written by someone other than the author, usually an industry leader, a celebrity, an expert, or a person of influence. Its sole purpose is to lend its author's credibility and authority to the book.

A foreword doesn't really contribute additional information about the subject matter; instead, it serves as a means of validating why the book was written and why the reader should read it. Imagine that you are standing in a bookstore and the book's cover has attracted you so that you pick it up. Or you are on-line and you've read the book description. Before taking the book to the checkout counter, or adding it to your cart, you turn to the foreword. Why? Because someone famous or someone whom you respect wrote it, and because the foreword will introduce the author, if this is someone who is not well known, as well as the significance of its subject matter.

What if you're the person who's been asked to write a foreword? What is your first step? You ask the author for a copy of the manuscript, of course. If you have the time and the interest, you read it. If not, at the very least, you skim the table of contents and read a chapter or two that capture your attention.

What should you cover in the foreword? The foreword is all about the book and its relevance or benefit to the reader. Share your expertise as it relates to the subject matter of the book. Your job is to give the reader some insight into how the book can help him, and why reading it should be important to him. You have the credibility; the reader will listen to you.

Be as specific as you are able. What prompted the reader to pick up the book in the first place? What problem will this book solve for the reader? How will the book benefit the reader? Give an overview of why the book is important. Answer these questions and you will have produced the quintessential foreword.

How does one accomplish this? You could write about a chapter in the book, about the book as a whole, or about the author's work, in general. You can write a short anecdote about something that happened in your life that relates — even loosely — to the book. Or you can write something that relates to the chapter you just read.

Say something about the author. Have you met? How long have you known each other (or known of each other)? Can you relate a personal anecdote about the author? You could discuss how the author's work has affected your life or the importance of the work you're introducing to the reader.

If you don't know the author personally, devote more space to the book's message. Talk about the relevance of the book or its subject matter, and wax enthusiastic about its validity.

It's your choice how you approach this. Just know that this is only one of two critical components. There is more to the ideal foreword. What's the other element?

Talk about yourself. Yes, you're well known. Yes, you may even be a celebrity. Yes, you have a reputation. But not everyone who picks up this book is aware of it. So, don't be modest. You were chosen to write the foreword because of your credibility and expertise; now is the time to flaunt it. Do not hesitate to remind people of why you are well known in the first place. Spend some time on this factor because it is your authority that makes your foreword effective.

Then wrap it up. If you really want to look like a pro, reference an idea from your opening paragraph again at the end to bring the foreword full circle.

How long should your foreword be? Aim for one thousand words. That's just one-to-three pages. A foreword does not have to be wordy to accomplish its purpose. In some ways, the shorter, the better. Powerful but concise is best.

What tone should you take in your foreword? What's the style? The tenor of a foreword should be friendly, chatty, personal, and relatable.

How does one end a foreword? Sign off on your foreword with your name, your title, the title of a recent book you have written or radio or television show you have hosted, or other significant data about yourself, the city where you live, and the date.

And you're done. You've stamped this work with the seal of your approval and you've made a difference, not just in the author's life, but also in the lives of all of those readers who would not have chosen this book but for you!

* * *

I include this here because, as I have advised earlier, the lawyer looking for someone to write the foreword to his book should be prepared to write the first draft of it for the foreword author. Apply the rules included here and you'll have a foreword of which you can be proud. Then send some version of these instructions to your foreword author if he's never written one before. We've all read books but few of us realize the elements that comprise a truly outstanding foreword.

BUILD BUZZ FOR YOUR BOOK

Once you've written your book, build excitement in its debut by staging book releases, as well as including a preorder period. This is similar to a coming attraction for a movie that builds excitement before the work is even released. Not only will you begin to sell copies of your book before it is released, but, if you stage it well, there will likely be renewed enthusiasm for your prior books.

Prior to the release, reveal segments of your book on your blog, website, or social media platform. Such samples will drive preorder sales. When you do this, always notify readers of the release date and how they can order the book (your call to action).

At the same time, remind them that your prior books are available now for purchase. Hold contests to give away books to lucky readers. Run promotions for those who purchase early or buy more than one of your books.

Place your book on preorder using Smashwords, which distributes preorders to Apple iBooks, Barnes & Noble, and Kobo. Preorders allow you to accept orders prior to the release date, thereby allowing you to accumulate sales before the book is even released. Why is this important? Not only does it build a buzz around your book, but it will get you a higher placement on bestseller charts before the book even goes on sale. It is important to rank as high as possible on those lists because it will give you more visibility and credibility when you do launch.

Preorders help you to capture your reader's attention as soon as your book comes across their radar. They can immediately preorder the book, rather than having to remember to order it when it is finally released.

By releasing your book early, you give merchandising managers greater flexibility to promote your book. And, if they notice a large volume of preorders, they are more likely to promote your book further.

Follow these steps to set up a preorder on Smashwords:

- Once your book is complete and formatted for Smashwords, click to the Smashwords Publish page.
- Click "Make it a Preorder." Select a release date that is about a month away.
- Upload your book. (If you need to update your book during the preorder period, simply upload the new version via your dashboard.)

- Check for Auto Vetter errors.
- Download epub with Adobe Digital Editions, and check that your formatting is correct.
- Once your book is listed for preorder, begin marketing by providing your fans direct links to the preorder pages. Consider giving your readers incentive to purchase the book early, like offering it at a reduced rate. Or offering a coupon code. And don't forget to mention your other books!

Proactively market your book as early as possible. Part of that task, of course, is to market yourself. The more people know who you are, the more books you will sell. So, make sure that you are highly visible on social media. Set time aside each day to post to your social media accounts. Also, make it easy for people to connect with you on social media by making your social media addresses as visible as possible. List them in your books, on your business cards, on your website, on your blogs, on your social media accounts, etc. Blog and/or participate actively on Twitter and LinkedIn.

Make sure that common search terms for your subject matter lead to your book. Publish hyperlinks on your blog or website that point to your Smashwords profile. To maximize your search engine optimization, link many sites to your Smashwords profile. Do a Smashwords interview. Write reviews of other Smashwords authors, which creates a hyperlink back to your author page. Invite other authors to join you at Smashwords. They will bring their fans with them, which means more possible fans for your books, as well.

Tell everyone you know about your book, including your social media connections. Provide them with a direct hyperlink to your Smashwords profile. Tell your readers how they can connect with you. Make it easy for them by providing many options by being present on many different social media platforms.

Don't forget to publish your press release about your book's release. See *Write Attention-Grabbing Press Releases,* at page 83.

Create a PowerPoint book trailer for your book, upload it to SlideShare.net, and then embed it in your website, blog, and social media accounts. By engaging different senses than those that a textual book engages, you appeal to different sensory levels, like sight and sound. People are more likely to act when they are engaged on various sensory levels. For the same reason, consider leveraging YouTube videos to reach your potential readers.

You worked so hard on your book. Now that you're about to publish it, reap the rewards of high sales by marketing your book to its fullest!

WRITE ATTENTION-GRABBING PRESS RELEASES

A press release is a written statement to the media. It is an inexpensive, easy way to obtain publicity for your practice. It can also be used to generate a feature story. Reporters are more likely to consider a story idea if they first receive your press release.

It is important to appeal to the audience of the publication in which you would like to be published. As always, develop an avatar of your perfect reader, and write directly to her.

There are any number of tips for preparing catchy press releases. There's no question that grabbing the press' attention is both a science and an art.

Start strong to grab the reader's attention. Begin with a one-sentence headline that includes your firm's name. The length of your headline varies based on the search engine: Google is 60 characters; Yahoo is 120 characters; and PRWeb is 170 characters.

To appear more credible, do not use all bold, caps, or explanation points in your heading. Instead, capitalize every word except for prepositions and articles of three characters or less. This is the sentence that will draw the reader in or cause him to move on to the next release. So be creative, yet keep it simple and clear. Extract the most important words from your release, and build your headline using those words in a logical, attention-grabbing fashion. Make sure that you use keywords that people are likely to use when searching for the information that you are providing. Write your headline after you have drafted your press release to be sure that you include the most important keywords and information.

Once the headline is created, the rest of the release should abide by these rules:

- The first paragraph should summarize your release. It should be one to four sentences.
- The dateline and lead paragraph together answer who, what, when, where, and why. An editor may only read this "key elements" paragraph, so hit on all of your important points. Avoid using a lot of adjectives. It should be a maximum of 25 words. Include important keywords.
- The body of the release should include more detail while still appealing to your audience to read further. Do not be verbose. The body should only be 300-800 words. Be neutral and objective. Provide details about the information that you are sharing. Keep sentences and paragraphs short, about three to four lines per

paragraph. Press releases are short, so you must inform your audience in an interesting, yet concise way. Choose your words wisely. Use real life examples to illustrate how your services solve a problem. Don't be afraid to brag a little bit. Do not include an e-mail address or create link spam.

- Don't forget to include your contact information, and if necessary, boilerplate and safe harbor language.
- Ensure that your subject is newsworthy by emphasizing the points that are interesting to the publisher's audience, not just the facts that you want to tell them. Press releases are appropriate in the following situations: announcing a new service; publishing a book; winning an award; presenting a workshop; hosting a seminar; announcing a new employee, etc.
- Include a good hook by tying your information to current events, recent studies, relevant social issues, etc.
- Always include a "call to action" so that your reader knows what you want him to do.
- Include a quote from a reputable source that will be available to give further comments, if requested to do so.
- Write in the third person, and use the past tense. Use active voice.
- Avoid jargon because it will limit your reading audience.
- Write professionally to establish credibility. Proofread your release to ensure that it is free of sloppy errors.
- Place the most important information at the beginning.
- Do not exceed one page.
- Use anchor text and hyperlinks to point readers back to your site.
- Do not use HTML.
- Keep even spacing.
- Avoid special characters.
- Limit in-text links to one link per 100 words.
- Convert charts and graphs to images or PDFs.

Conclude your press release with a brief summary. Signal the end of the press release with three hash symbols centered directly underneath the last line of the release.

Your press release should look like a story. Use good grammar, proper spelling, and the correct formatting. Make sure that the editor doesn't have to fix your mistakes or perform additional research. Write a press release that is close to the way the editor will actually publish it, and it may see publication with minimal editing.

Research the editors whom you would like to publish your release. Appeal to them directly, and personalize your release to each of them. Make sure that each one's publication is appropriate for your release and that its readers would be interested in your topic.

Also, research and follow their editorial and submission guidelines.

E-mail the release with the headline as the subject and the release as the body of the e-mail, and not as an attachment. You don't want to waste the editor's time by asking him to click on an attachment, and he isn't likely to do it, either. Follow up with a phone call, once sufficient time has passed for the editor to have reviewed your release.

A well-written, interesting press release is a great way to publicize your law practice! I include a sample here in Appendix 4.

Write Must-Follow Blogs

Blogging is an essential task for anyone who wants to establish a reputation as a force to be reckoned with in a certain field. But posting regular blogs can be intimidating, especially if you don't fancy yourself a writer. However, if you set aside one hour for each of three days every week, you will soon have the content you need to become a blogger.

When blogging, be authentic, and speak in your true voice. You will be blogging often, so, if you are not genuine, it will eventually become obvious. In that case, your readers will not trust you and they will lose interest.

Allow your readers to know who you are, what you stand for, and what your goals are. Don't be afraid to say something provocative, even if you may upset somebody. You can never make everyone happy, so, instead, gain your readers' trust by stating your actual, un-sugarcoated opinion. Consider campaigning politicians who speak from both sides of their mouths. Nobody trusts them. Don't be like them. Instead, ensure that your message always reflects your personal brand.

Coming up with fresh blog topics can be challenging, but not when you keep your ear to the ground. My protégés always ask me the best questions to which I never know the "right" answers, but that, too, is an opportunity to co-author an article blog that we bounce back-and-forth via e-mail like a tennis ball to flesh out before publishing. And, of course, when I myself conduct a workshop, the audience and I always come up with marvelous subjects on which I will later write.

There are other methods of identifying valuable blog topics. Use Google keywords or phrases to spark ideas. Find out what people want to know, and then inform them about it. Go to AVVO and look at the questions that folks have posted there for lawyers to answer. Find practice area experts, ask them questions on Twitter, and when they respond, blog about what top experts say about the matter. Feature the experts in your article.

Always remember that your purpose in blogging is to:

1. Educate your readers so that your blog is the go-to source for information for those who need you;
2. Provide interesting content to keep readers coming back; and
3. Increase your own search engine optimization so that those who need you can find you easily.

Create a weekly editorial calendar so that you have a plan for your blog schedule. For example, on Mondays, you might respond to frequently asked questions. On Wednesdays, you might blog a case study about an interesting matter that you have had and the lessons you learned from it. On Fridays, you could post a roundup of news, articles, and interesting links that you've found during the week that would be useful or informative to your readers. While most of these should focus on issues specific to your practice area or profession, about a quarter of the time, throw in an inspirational or funny one.

When writing blogs, write copy that can be scanned by the reader. Use subheads, bullet points, lists, and bolded copy to help your readers easily focus on the main points without having to read every word.

Include an image (preferably two) for every post. It makes the copy easier for the reader to scan and makes it simpler to share on all levels. And more attractive; we all like pictures.

Blogs should be 400 to 800 words each so that they are long enough for search engines to scan and short enough to keep readers' attention. That said, mine tend to be longer and more recent studies now suggest that as many as 2000 words will optimize the likelihood that readers looking for your content will be able to find you. So, check the current school of thought on that issue when you start writing.

In each blog, include one or two relevant links to other blog posts or pages on your site. Also include external links every 100 to 200 words. (Ensure that those links don't take your readers away from your blog, but, instead, simply open in a new window.)

Don't forget to share your posts with your social media discussion groups. And include those discussion groups pertinent to law.

Finally, don't forget to engage your audience so they keep coming back to hear more of what you have to say. Encourage them to comment, and when they do, always respond. Learn about your readers by looking at their social media accounts. Build relationships with them, and show that you care what they say. Make them feel special, and they will be more likely to share your blogs. Always keep in mind who your reader is, and speak to her as though you are having a conversation with a friend.

Ask everyone in your family and your practice to follow you. The more followers you have, the higher your optimization. Offer to follow them if they have a blog, as well. "What goes around comes around." And, by the way, follow me so that I can follow you. www.OpenPalmLaw.com/blog/.

WRITE COMPELLING TWEETS

Writing a compelling tweet can be challenging; you have a limited number of characters (140) with which to make your point. To increase your likelihood of re-tweets, the optimum number of characters for a tweet is between 71 and 100; that is long enough to get your point across, but short enough that the re-tweeter can also comment.

The rules for writing compelling tweets are not what you would think. Your sole goal in a tweet is to convince someone to click on it.

- Pique your reader's interest so that she wants to learn more.
- Make her curious.
- Tease her.
- Be vague; it stimulates a need in your reader to solve the mystery you have posed. To what are you referring?
- Instead of nouns, use words like "these," "this," and "it."
- Purposely omit information.
- Keep your tweets conversational without sounding professional or using jargon.
- Be funny or inspiring.

The most viral words and phrases include:

- Imperative words that tell you to do something;
- Visual words like "video" and "picture";
- Superlatives like "the best" or "the most";
- Audience-referencing phrases like those using "you"; and
- How-to phrases.

Specifically ask followers to retweet. Include more adverbs and verbs than nouns and adjectives; action words will compel your readers to do something.

People prefer to read tweets in which each word is capitalized, rather than those in which all letters are lower case or all capitalized. This format sets off the content and signifies that it is something special that your followers will want to read and share.

Use hashtags. They should be short, recognizable to your followers, and allow them to follow easily. Don't use more than two in any given tweet. Choose them wisely and in a way that will add the most value to your followers.

Use links, images, photos, and videos to engage your followers more and increase your retweets. Use a URL shortener (like bit.ly or ow.ly) so that you don't have to use as many characters.

As always, decide who your reader is. Then determine when the best time is to post your tweet. When are your followers most likely to have time to read it and to be somewhere where they can read it? Are other lawyers more likely to read your tweets during working hours on a weekday? Or would they be more likely to read during their leisure time on the weekends?

The more you tweet, the more you'll be re-tweeted. Be consistent with the frequency and times of your tweets so that your followers can depend on them. Tweet enough so that you are being noticed but not so often that your content becomes stale. You always want your content to be fresh.

To determine when and how often you should tweet, measure your growth. How many followers do you get each day? How many actually interact with you? How many re-tweet your posts or click on your links?

When re-tweeting, always add something original of your own. By putting your own words in front of the tweet, you get credit for saying it yourself. But don't just re-tweet. You should be tweeting your own content, as well.

Compose your Twitter bio in the first person. Be funny, truthful, and interesting.

Ask everyone in your family and practice to follow you and offer to follow them back. And follow me so that I can follow you. I am @OpenPalmLaw. ☺

Top Tips for Creating Effective Infomercials

When I say the word "infomercial," your first thought may be of an extended television program that was always on late at night when you were having difficulty sleeping. These allegedly promoted a product or service in an informative and objective way when there was nothing else on TV and we were captive to the program.

But I'm not talking about infomercials that you can catch on television during the wee hours of the night, although they are amazingly effective and you may want to use some of the same pitching strategies as they do. I am talking about a brief, one-minute video on a specific subject that you can post on your website and on YouTube. You only have a limited time, so you'll need to make a big impact quickly. Follow these tips for creating a memorable infomercial:

1. First, begin with a relatable question or a bold statement about services you provide in order to catch the viewer's attention.
2. Next, back up that relatable question or bold statement with factual documentation that gives you credibility.
3. Then, explain to the viewer how the assertion in your bold statement affects them and why they should care.
4. Continue with how your services answer the relatable question or solve the problem identified in your bold statement.
5. Many infomercials repeat catchy slogans that viewers will remember long after they have watched your infomercial. "But wait, there's more!" "Set it, and forget it!" Give some thought to a slogan that might make sense for your practice area. A personal injury lawyer who started practice in Tampa has a catchphrase nearly everyone in the country now knows, "For the People." His slogan is so powerful that his firm has offices in many states now.
6. Finally, (I know I'm not surprising you when I say) finish with your call to action. What would you like the viewer to do? Call you for a consultation? Introduce you to a new referral partner? Tell a family member or a friend about the legal services you provide? Buy your book? Consider offering an incentive to entice the viewer into taking that action immediately.
7. Each week, record a new infomercial, and begin with a different jarring statistic. Don't say the same thing the same way every time.

8. Post each infomercial on YouTube and on your website. Then tweet about it and post it on Facebook and on LinkedIn. Are there discussion groups on topics that interest your target clients or referral partners to which you can also post it? Do that.

For some sample infomercials that I use as a family lawyer marketing out-of-court divorce work, see Appendix 12.

Present

INTRODUCTION TO PRESENTATION FORTES

Think about the people in your community who are constantly being invited to speak at seminars and events, and to interview on podcasts, on radio shows, and on television. What do you think of these people? You probably consider them to be the authorities in their areas of practice, and your colleagues probably feel the same way. How did these people build their reputations as being the "go to" presenters in your area? These folks are able to communicate their missions and visions persuasively. They likely have a keen ability to connect with a crowd and a passion for their practice area. That enthusiasm is contagious and makes for a great speaker who is repeatedly asked back to present.

People who present often gain reputations as experts in their fields, what I call "influencers" or "champions." They attract more clients as word spreads of their respected standing in the community.

In this chapter, you will learn how to find venues in which to present, how to be invited to present, and how to decide what to present. You'll learn how to write and deliver your media pitch so that you are more likely to be asked to appear on television and radio.

You'll learn how to write and prepare for a presentation, from the introduction to the conclusion. You'll even get tips on how to survive a Q & A session.

You'll learn how to develop your own unique personal speaking style, whether it's jovial, serious, or falls somewhere in between. I'll explain how to create a PowerPoint and other helpful presentation aids. You'll receive common presenting tips, as well as errors and how to avoid them.

You'll learn how to read body language and what to do when an audience member displays negative body language. You'll learn how your own body language can affect a presentation and how your audience may react to it. You'll learn how to improve your body language to make you a more polished presenter. Learn how to get ready for a presentation, and how to use PowerPoint and how to engage your audience when you do present.

A speakers' bureau is a core group of speakers who are available for community meetings or gatherings. In this section, you will find speakers' bureau guidelines, protocols, forms, and instructions. You'll learn why establishing or joining a speakers' bureau is a critical opportunity to raise your own profile and to market your practice. Creating your own speakers' bureau offers not just an opportunity to educate the public and to act as a community resource, but also to raise your own visibility in the community.

I will instruct you how to issue a press release for your speaking events so that you have as big an audience as possible for your presentations.

The information contained in this section will help you present your way to becoming an influencer!

Presentation Basics

Are you confident in communicating your mission and your vision persuasively, to "spread the word" to more than one person at a time? The more knowledge you have about your subject, the more confident you will be.

Speak to groups. Guest on podcasts. Appear on radio and TV.

- Ask friends who belong to groups if they need speakers.
- Contact podcast interviewers and offer to guest on their podcast.
- Call professionals who host TV and radio shows and offer to appear.
- Follow up on your press releases with media marketing personnel.
- Send out your media pitch.

Develop your media pitch:

1. Intro
2. Platform
3. Thoughts
4. Close

Typical order of a speaking event:

1. Introduction
   a. Tell them what you're going to tell them.
   b. Start strong with a shocking fact, a funny joke, or an inspiring quote so that you capture their attention immediately.
2. Body
   a. Tell them.
   b. Repeat your important points. You don't need many key points. Three is sufficient; four is arguably too many. Keep the message simple, not simplistic.
   c. Be cognizant of your time limit.
3. Q & A
   a. Answer the question.

   b. If you don't know the answer to a question, tell the inquirer that you will look into it and contact him directly with the answer.
   c. Consider whether to ask your audience if anyone in it knows the answer.
4. Conclusion
   a. Remind them what you told them.
   b. Decide on the ending before you start writing. Then aim for your goal.
   c. Finish strong, tying your conclusion to something that you said in your introduction.

Develop a personal speaking style.

- Be enthusiastic and informative.
- Speak loudly and clearly.
- Don't lecture. Be conversational.
- Joke only if you are comfortable doing so and it is appropriate. Humor is much easier and more natural for most folks, but, again, only if appropriate.
- Use the room, but don't pace.
- Look your audience in the eyes.
- Avoid fidgeting, mumbling, and slouching.
- Talk in threes because short term memory handles information better in segments of three to four, like three reasons, three tips, three bullet points, etc.

PRESENTATION TIPS

- Prepare! The more prepared you are, the more comfortable you'll be. Have a clear idea of what your key messages are. Include the latest research and findings to keep your presentation fresh.
- Establish rapport with the audience early. Tell a personal story. Make eye contact. Be likeable.
- Know your subject matter, including recent changes. Be clear about your message.
- Practice! Practice in front of a mirror. Record yourself and play it back. Does your voice sound enthusiastic? If not, fix that. Practice in front of friends and family. Be open to their critiques.
- Develop your personal style. Speak loudly and clearly. Be confident and enthusiastic.
- Know your audience, including their race, gender, ethnicity, and education level. Ensure that the subject matter is relevant to them.
- Only tell jokes if your subject matter is suitable and joking is appropriate to the audience, and if you are comfortable doing so. Natural humor is easier than jokes for most of us to employ, but, again, be careful that you

don't accidentally insult your audience.

- Know what is expected of you. How formal do you need to be? What technology and aids are you expected to use, if any? What is the appropriate dress?
- Be cognizant of time. Do not start early or end late.
- Know your venue. Can you walk around? Does it have the capability of supporting your technology? Is it so large that you will need a microphone? Is there easy parking, or should you arrive extra early?
- Arrive early to avoid unnecessary stress.
- Perform relaxation techniques before your presentation like breathing, listening to music, or exercising.
- Have water readily available.
- Use technology and props only if you are comfortable doing so. But don't be dependent upon them.
- Become comfortable with PowerPoint or similar programs because it will improve your overall presentation. Employ visuals (cartoons, photos, and diagrams) to enhance your audience's ability to recall your message.
- Tell stories.
- Employ film clips, when relevant. Same reason.
- Employ handouts to help visual learners absorb your subject matter. Additionally, most people want something that they can take with them. If they do, it helps to create the impression that they received something of value.
- Enroll in a public speaking class.
- Attend other presentations, and note what you like. Emulate it. Note what you don't like, and avoid doing it.
- Be passionate.
- Ask your audience questions; involve them in the event. Even if they don't raise their hands, considering how they would respond involves them.
- Study body language and employ it.
- Give goodies/gifts.
- Supply 3x5 blank cards at tables for questions – ask guests to include their names on the cards so that you can call them by name.
- Smile!

PRESENTATION ERRORS

- Not starting strong.
- Apologizing and self-criticizing.
- Criticizing others.
- Reading directly from notes or slides.
- Speaking in monotone.
- Speaking too slowly or too quickly.

- Using props and technology with which you are not comfortable.
- Using too many slides or slides with too much information and/or font that is too small.
- Telling inappropriate jokes.
- Cursing.
- Lecturing.
- Mumbling.
- Slouching.
- Fidgeting.
- Pacing.
- Turning your back on the audience.

Create a speakers' bureau.

A speakers' bureau is a core group of speakers who can knowledgeably discuss a topic, both with the professionals and the public. The purpose is to provide a panel of speakers who are available to educate both the public, as well as other professionals, and to arrange for appropriate speaking engagements for those speakers in various venues across the community.

Now what?

When you've arranged to present, then what? Create PowerPoints. Pull together some handouts. Include personal stories of your successes. And issue press releases about your speaking events. Write articles, blog, and tweet about it.

THE PARTS OF A PRESENTATION

Your presentations should be comprised of the following parts:

1. An opening that draws in the listener;
2. A preview of what's to come ("Tell them what you're going to tell them");
3. The body of the presentation ("Tell them");
4. Interaction with the audience;
5. A summary of what the audience should have learned ("Tell them what you told them"); and
6. A closing that leaves the audience inspired and wanting more, and that includes a call to action.

OPENING

Your opening sets the stage for your entire presentation, so it is imperative that you start strong. Tell a heartwarming or motivational tale, a funny story, a shocking statistic, or a jarring fact. Or begin with an activity that includes some or all of your audience, like having everyone respond to several questions that will elicit responses to lead you into your presentation. Your audience should immediately feel happy that they came and ready to learn more. You are setting the tone for the rest of your presentation, so be sure to command the room! Your opening should also include the following: 1) a greeting to the audience; 2) a self-introduction; and 3) an introduction of your topic.

PREVIEW

Briefly explain your agenda so that your audience knows what to expect. Also, give important instructions, for example, if interaction is encouraged, and what behavior should be avoided, like cell phone use. Set the stage, and take the lead!

BODY

The body is the meat of your presentation and should be the lengthiest portion. Demonstrate your expertise. Include everything of value, everything that the audience should consider, and everything of which you want your audience to be convinced.

INTERACTION

It is important to interact with your audience, rather than to simply lecture at them. ("Talking heads" are déclassé.) That is how your audience will get the most out of your presentation, and it will keep them interested, especially in lengthier presentations. Interact with them as much as possible during all phases.

Beware of hecklers who want to trip you up for their own entertainment. Shut them down as quickly and as politely as possible.

Before even going on stage, interact positively with as much of your audience as possible. Say "hello," shake hands, and make small talk. The more people with whom you interact positively, the more people who will want you to do well during your presentation. I'll never forget one of my favorite professors in college who started the first day by sitting at a desk as though he was a student, interacting with as many real students as possible. When the bell rang, he stood up and began teaching, and we were all shocked that this young man was our professor. He made a great impression early on, and that very quickly set the mood for the entire semester.

SUMMARY

Briefly recap your entire presentation. Highlight the most important concepts. As you go, ask your audience if they have questions. Continue to interact with them.

CONCLUSION

Just as you began, end on a strong note. Tie your conclusion to your introduction. As you are writing your opening, plan your closing. You want your audience walking away feeling that the time they spent with you was valuable. Be memorable and compelling.

Prepare for Your Presentation

Be sure that you understand the objective of your presentation. Record it in writing, and continue to ask yourself, "What else?" What elements must I include to make it a success? What is your "call to action?"

Do your homework ahead of time. What is currently compelling about this topic? Are there recent advances that I should discuss? Are there any hot button issues that I should avoid?

Consider the make-up of your audience. It is important to know their average education and their understanding of the particular topic, so that you are speaking at their level. You should also be aware of their genders, races, and ages because they may mean differences in their interests. If you are speaking on a more controversial topic, you will want to know your audience's general position on the topic so that you don't offend.

It is also important to know the number of people to whom you will present. Your interaction will vary depending on whether you are speaking to a smaller, more intimate crowd, or to a larger, less personal crowd. Also, you are likely to prepare differently, from a mental perspective, depending on the size of your crowd. A larger crowd may be more intimidating due to the number of eyes staring at you.

Before you begin preparing, research your venue. How big is it? How are the tables and chairs set up? How are the lighting, sound, and technology?

Additionally, ensure that you understand your time constraints. Don't prepare a two-hour presentation for a one-hour block of time. Be sure to have some time fillers in case you blow through your presentation too quickly or don't command the audience interaction that you expected.

Who are the other presenters and on what topics are they presenting? Be sure to avoid redundancy.

Write a brief outline in bullet-point format. Brainstorm, and quickly jot down everything that comes to mind. Don't worry about grammar, punctuation, or whether something is a good idea or relevant. Just get all your initial thoughts down on paper. Then, review your outline, removing items that are not appropriate, and expanding on those that are. Make sure that your objective and message are clear and different. Your objective is what you want your audience to take from your presentation. Your message is what you put into your presentation that provides a clear benefit to your audience.

Finally, always practice your presentation. No matter how confident a presenter you are, the more you practice, the better you will be. Videotape yourself or present in front of a mirror so that you know how you look and can eliminate any distracting habits you might have developed. Ask your friends to watch and critique you, as well.

You should know your material so well that, if your technology fails you, you will still be able to proceed. Also, think of possible questions that will be posed, and have responses ready. Once you have done several dry runs of your presentation, keep practicing the parts where you stumbled.

On the day of your presentation, give yourself enough time to arrive at the venue early so as not to add any unnecessary stress. This will also give you time to perform relaxation techniques, to practice empowering stances (read *Consider Body Language*, at page 111), and to arm yourself with the right mindset in which to deliver a stellar presentation.

USING POWERPOINT

First things first. Ensure that your venue has the capability for you to utilize a PowerPoint presentation. These days, most venues will, but smaller ones may not. You don't want to prepare for a presentation, expecting to use your PowerPoint, only to discover that you cannot. (By the way, if you cannot, there's no rule against handing out printed copies of your PowerPoint, if you already have one, and using it anyway.)

To create a professional PowerPoint, use a consistent theme, color, font, and size on each page. But make sure that the color and theme you choose is not distracting. I like to use my Open Palm watermark, very pale, in the background of my slides, with a personalized full-color teal swoosh at the bottom of each slide, below any text or pictures on the slide.

While you can certainly use sentence fragments, make sure your spelling, grammar, and punctuation are correct.

Many new presenters will put the entire presentation on their slides. Don't do this! It will cause you to just read straight from the slides, to forget to interact with your audience, and frankly, to bore them to death. Instead, use no more than four to six bullet points per slide with no more than four to six words per bullet point. (You can put more detailed information in your own private notes that will show up for only you with each slide, but don't include too much material on each slide or you'll fall into the same trap of just reading right from your PowerPoint.)

Better still, use more images than words on your slides and put all the words into your notes.

For the same reasons, don't include too many slides. You should have no more than two slides per minute of your presentation. That being said, you should usually include the following slides:

- An opening slide with the title of your presentation and your professional information;
- A slide displaying the objective of your presentation;
- An agenda slide;
- Slides that follow your agenda, referring back to it as informative headings, and providing more succinct information in bullet points, or with visual interests like pictures and graphs;
- A slide that recaps the purpose;
- A slide that recaps the agenda;

- A slide for questions and answers; and
- A closing slide with the presentation title, your information, and ways to connect to you and your business.

That said, if you only have half an hour to present, which has happened to me, don't waste your time with anything not directly related to your topic. Just make sure that the person who introduces you has the bio you want her to read. You will find such a short PowerPoint presentation included here in Appendix 13. (I'm so sorry it's in black & white; it was a lot prettier in person!) I've included it with my notes section, so that you can see exactly what I mean about slides versus words.)

Don't use your technology as a crutch. Look at your audience, and not at your PowerPoint. Your technology should simply enhance your presentation, making it more interesting for the visual learners in your audience. Be sufficiently prepared so that if your technology fails you (that never happens, right?!), you can still give a powerful presentation.

ENGAGE YOUR AUDIENCE

We've all attended presentations where the presenter just droned on and on incessantly, like a broken record. Who can forget economics teacher, Ben Stein, from *Ferris Bueller's Day Off*:

> In 1930, the Republican-controlled House of Representatives, in an effort to alleviate the effects of the . . . Anyone? Anyone? the Great Depression, passed the . . . Anyone? Anyone? The tariff bill? The Hawley-Smoot Tariff Act? Which, anyone? Raised or lowered? . . . raised tariffs, in an effort to collect more revenue for the federal government. Did it work? Anyone? Anyone know the effects? It did not work, and the United States sank deeper into the Great Depression. Today we have a similar debate over this. Anyone know what this is? Class? Anyone? Anyone? Anyone seen this before? The Laffer Curve. Anyone know what this says? It says that at this point on the revenue curve, you will get exactly the same amount of revenue as at this point. This is very controversial. Does anyone know what Vice President Bush called this in 1980? Anyone? Something-d-o-o economics. "Voodoo" economics. Bueller? . . . Bueller? . . . Bueller? Bueller? Bueller? Bueller?

You may wonder why I included *all* of this incredibly boring speech here. It's because it was *so* funny that many people don't realize how long Ben Stein droned on and on . . . and on. Obviously, the teacher was not getting the interaction that he wanted from his students. Have you ever felt like this when giving a presentation? It's not a good feeling. But by following these tips, you can get the type of responses that you want.

Ask questions for input. Ferris' teacher did that, but not in a way that actually elicited responses. Although he was asking, "Anyone?" it was just part of his long, monotonous speech. Instead, using inflections in your voice and enthusiasm, ask questions, and wait for responses, while looking your audience in the eyes. When you do get a response, listen carefully, and ask appropriate follow up questions. Engage your audience in a discussion as if you were chatting with them at a cocktail party.

Avoid distractions like a dull, droning voice, noisy jewelry, and shoes that loudly click-clack. If you've recorded yourself presenting, then you can avoid tics that most speakers suffer from, whether it's putting your hands in your pockets, or twisting your wedding ring on your finger, or swaying from side-to-side. They are distracting and you need to take steps to avoid those.

Also, make sure that your technology is not diverting your audience's attention by following the tips in *Using PowerPoint, supra*.

Pass each of your handouts out *when each handout will be used* so that people do not look at them, and ignore you, when you are on a different topic. Then give them a moment to look at it before proceeding.

Break up your presentation by including small group activities like table discussions.

Further, tell your audience early on that you will take questions throughout your presentations. Ask often if there are any questions. Remember that how you respond to your first question will be an indicator for whether people will feel comfortable asking more questions.

When an audience member asks a question, do not respond "Great question!" or something similar, because if you don't say that to the next person with a question, they might assume that you think their question is silly, and they might be discouraged from continuing to interact.

When a question is asked, repeat it so that you are sure that you understood correctly and so that the rest of the audience can hear the question. Think before you respond so that you show the audience that you respect the audience member enough to give his question sufficient thought, and so that you offer a thoughtful response. Once you have completed your response, ask whether you addressed the asker's question to ensure that he is satisfied.

If you do not know the answer, simply be truthful, and let the asker know that you will research his question and get back to him.

Before the end of your presentation, always include time for Q & A.

Finally, speak with your audience, and not at them or to your PowerPoint. Most importantly, let your enthusiasm for your subject shine through.

CREATE LIFE-CHANGING PRESENTATIONS

Have you ever attended a presentation where the speaker's words resonated so deeply that you left feeling compelled to change your life's course immediately? The speaker was enthusiastic and knowledgeable. The material was cutting edge and exciting.

So how can you give a life-altering presentation like that?

When preparing a presentation, remember that your audience is looking for guidance, hope, and inspiration. Set up speaking engagements where you expect to make an impact, at law schools, colleges, young professional organizations, and solo practitioner organizations. Also at organizations that are related in some way to your topic or practice area. These may be service, charitable, professional, business, legal, religious, or otherwise.

Promote your speaking engagement so that you fill the seats and so that your students become excited about your upcoming presentation. Send e-mails with information about the event, and advertise on social media or with on-line advertisements. Advertise the old-fashioned way in newspapers, magazines, on bulletin boards, in newsletters, etc. Pass out tickets to your affiliates who can hand them out to their contacts who might benefit from the information you will provide.

While you must provide knowledge, it is your enthusiasm and compassion that will turn an everyday presentation into one that might change an attendee's life. Tell engaging and relatable personal stories. Be a good storyteller. Use your space to move around. Speak using vocal inflection. Don't force jokes into your presentation; simply allow your natural humor to shine through. Smile. Look your audience in the eyes. Create ways for them to interact with you rather than just lecturing them.

During breaks, speak one-to-one with especially interested students.

Remember that audience members will learn best in different ways. Some are visual learners who understand information best if they see it. Some are more audio-focused and take information best that they hear. And some are kinesthetic because they absorb information by what they feel.

Appeal to each of these senses. Use a PowerPoint or something similar to appeal to the visual learners, play soft music for the audio learners, and provide handouts for the kinesthetic learners. But don't forget about our senses of smell and taste. Offer snacks with comforting aromas like fresh-baked treats that will melt in your listeners' mouths.

Begin your presentation by answering why you are passionate about what you present. Answering "Why?" early in your presentation will motivate your audience to action.

Finally, to be life changing, your audience must respect that you are knowledgeable in the subject you choose to present. A great way to convey knowledge is by having authored a book on your subject. Not only will you learn more about your subject during your writing process, but also once you have published your book, you will be viewed as an expert in your field.

Always end on a high note. Thank your audience for attending, and praise them for the work that they are already doing to advance your message. Always offer them a call to action. And remind them that they can always come to you with questions. End with a personal anecdote that will resonate with them even after you have left the room.

Imagine the satisfaction you will have when, years from now, your former audience member thanks you for the impact that your presentation had on his career and on his life.

CONSIDER BODY LANGUAGE

Have you ever attended a conference where you could not focus on what was being said because of *how* the speaker presented during the program? Who can forget when future republican presidential candidate, Marco Rubio, took a swig mid-speech from a small water bottle during his GOP State of the Union rebuttal? Such a small gesture made him appear nervous, caused his audience to lose faith in what he was saying, and encouraged people to wonder if the senator had just botched his chances of one day becoming President of the United States.

Whether you present to a room of 500 or to a consultation of one, your body language is the most impactful factor on your audience. Body language is 55% of the speaker's total influence, with voice at 38%, and words at only 7%.

Renowned social psychologist, Amy Cuddy,[4] performed an experiment on how nonverbal expressions of power (i.e., expansive, open, space-occupying postures) affect people's feelings, behaviors, and hormone levels. According to Cuddy, just as animals open up and make themselves appear larger to show power and dominance, people do the same when they enjoy power chronically or feel powerful.

Further, regardless of whether people are born with or without sight, when they feel pride, they make similar motions of reaching their arms up in a "V" and lifting their chins. It is simply human nature to express our joy by spreading our arms high and wide, as if about to hug the entire world.

By contrast, when we feel powerless, both animals and humans close up to make themselves look smaller.

When a high-power person meets with a low-power individual, rather than mirror one another, they do exactly the opposite. So, if you view someone as more powerful than you are, you make yourself smaller. Generally, women feel less powerful than men, so they tend to shrink.

This is why the phrase "fake it till you make it" is so effective. If you act in ways to *look* more powerful, you will *feel* more powerful. Powerful people take more risks, are more optimistic, are more confident, think more abstractly, have more of the dominance hormone (testosterone), and have less of the stress hormone (cortisol).

Cuddy and her colleagues performed an experiment in which they first obtained samples of the test subjects' saliva. Afterward, they arranged each subject in either a high

[4] *Your Body Language Shapes Who You Are*, TED Talks, 2012.

power or a low power pose for two minutes. Next, they offered the test subjects the opportunity to gamble. Finally, Cuddy took second saliva samples.

Of those who performed high power poses, 86% gambled; on the other hand, only 60% of the low power posers chose to gamble.

Those who performed high power poses increased their testosterone by 20% and decreased their cortisol by 25%. In contrast, low power posers exhibited a 10% decrease in testosterone and a 15% increase in cortisol.

Clearly, our non-verbal actions impact, not just how others think and feel, but also how we think and feel about *ourselves*. Why should legal professionals care about this, aside from the obvious, if we choose to market our practices by presenting outside the conference room?

1. Our bodies change our minds.
2. Our minds change our behavior.
3. Our behavior changes our outcome.

Legal professionals should share this information with their clients. Clients who adopt body postures associated with power and control for as little as two minutes before a deposition or a court hearing or a mediation will increase testosterone, decrease cortisol, increase appetite for risk, and cause better performance in both job interviews and negotiations. And you will, as well.

"Don't fake it till you make it. Fake it till you become it."

During any important event or meeting, mimic your power stance, when you can. Use good posture. Open your chest and arms to maximize air flow and also because, as explained above, power stances make us feel and look more powerful. This attitude will make you appear approachable and confident.

Smile. It will make you more likeable, inviting, and relatable.

Look your listeners in the eyes. Not only will you appear more trustworthy, but people will pay more attention to what you say. They will feel engaged and part of the conversation.

Your listeners will pay more attention to you if you vary your gestures. Make use of your entire anatomy, using your hands, your arms, your head, and your body. Use both small motions and large gestures. Use positive motions like nodding your head and mirroring your listener's movements. Your gestures should always emphasize your point.

What should you not do? Avoid flailing to the point of distraction. Avoid fidgeting; you will seem nervous, and your listeners will pay more attention to your twitching and less to the point that you are making. Avoid crossing your arms; you will appear defensive. Avoid crossing your legs; you will look nervous and unprofessional.

If you use a whiteboard, never turn your back to your audience while you speak, as you will appear rude, and you will lose their attention. If you want to draw attention to what you've written there, turn to the side and point with your finger or use a laser pointer.

Most importantly, when it comes to body language, just act as naturally as possible. If you try to use body language that doesn't feel natural, you will look stiff and uncomfortable, which will make you look untrustworthy.

So, next time you're at an important event or meeting, remember to take your best, most confident power pose for two minutes and drink your water *before* you enter the room; then act as naturally as possible once you do.

Create a Speakers' Bureau

A speakers' bureau is a core group of speakers who are available to speak at community meetings to educate the public on certain topics. The lay public benefits from the spread of valuable information. The speakers benefit because their profiles are raised in the communities in which they practice. But there are any number of decisions that must be made prior to putting yourself out there as the organizer of a bureau.

To create a speakers' bureau, first establish guidelines. (See Appendix 14 for sample guidelines, as well as an information sheet form.) What kind of speakers do you want? What type of training and how much of it do you require of your speakers? What steps must a speaker take to join the speakers' bureau?

Once on the speakers' bureau, what preparatory steps must your speakers take prior to their presentations? How far in advance must a speaker discuss his potential subjects with the bureau coordinator? Is the coordinator's approval required? By when must the speaker provide a summary of the presentation, his resume, handouts, and/or his PowerPoint? Is a speaker entitled to any reimbursements or compensation? May a speaker market his own practice during a presentation?

Speakers should be encouraged to address subjects about which they have direct and detailed knowledge, broad experience, formal training, and/or personal involvement. A speaker's ability to address a given subject is a combination of training and quality, length, and breadth of experience. Speakers should address subjects that will provide knowledge and training at all levels of experience on subjects that are dear to the hearts of the listening public. Prior to presentations, remind speakers to research their audiences so that they can speak at their levels, whatever they may be. A speaker at a jail will not address his audience the same way he would address a group of accountants.

Find a location for your speakers' bureau. While it may be based in your office, will presentations always be at the same place? Probably not. Your speakers should be available to travel to different locations like churches, schools, retirement homes, libraries, professional association meetings, and other law firms. Your speakers may also present on a regular basis at specific locations.

Consider whether you'd like to arrange for speakers to be available for television and radio appearances. Also, the more speakers you have, the more opportunities they will have to speak because you should use each of their networks, as well as your own, to gain speaking engagements. Always ask speakers in what organizations they themselves are involved, whether religious, professional, charitable, sports, service, or referral networking.

Encourage them to use their connections to obtain more speaking engagements for the bureau.

Always require speakers to provide questionnaires to the audience to evaluate the speaker's presentation. You can prepare a standard form for all of your speakers to use. I provide a sample audience feedback form in Appendix 11. Both positive and negative feedback will enable the speakers to become better presenters, which will result in a stronger speakers' bureau.

Volunteers will get so much out of presenting. Presenting helps the presenters become more knowledgeable about their topics for various reasons. As they prepare for their presentations, they review and update their own knowledge, ensuring that they know the latest developments. As they present, the topic becomes even more ingrained in their brain. As listeners ask questions, they are considering perspectives that they may not have considered and on which they may later perform more research.

Furthermore, a professional who is known as one who presents often will be viewed as an expert in the field; more individuals will want to retain her.

Finally, speakers who are permitted to market their firms during their presentations gain more recognition for their firms or offices, and more opportunity to attract clients of their legal services.

Profile

INTRODUCTION TO PROFILE FORTES

An intriguing profile will attract the right clients and professionals to your practice. You'll no longer be required to chase opportunities; instead, you can afford to be choosy about the opportunities that come your way. A compelling profile will encourage potential clients and colleagues to want to learn more about your mission, services, and uniqueness. Your profile should clearly reflect your mission and vision. It should be easy to find both on-line and in traditional media. You should constantly adapt it as your practice evolves.

Here, you'll learn how to grow your profile and use it to market your practice. I'll give you helpful tips on writing a mission statement and vision. You'll learn how to effectively combine high level industry information with easy-to-comprehend lay terminology so that you appeal to both potential clients and other professionals, as well as entice media to interview you about your cutting-edge firm. You'll learn how to appropriately communicate your personality so that it is easy for the reader to relate to you. You'll learn how to successfully demonstrate your firm's uniqueness.

I'll also explain how to most effectively use the most common social media websites, like Facebook, Twitter, and LinkedIn. You'll learn how to increase your connections on these websites and how to best utilize them. You'll learn how to successfully Tweet using only 140 characters. You'll receive tips for blogging and increasing your search engine optimization.

I'll explain the tremendous power of testimonials and how to obtain the ones that will attract new clients.

You'll receive general tips on improving your profile, as well as common errors people make that negatively impact their profile and how to correct them. In short, you'll understand the power of your profile, and how to maximize that power for the benefit of your practice.

PROFILE BASICS

Your personal brand should be conspicuous, visible, and easily identified, both online and in traditional media. Here are the steps to making that happen, in a nutshell. (You'll find more on each of these basics inside.)

First, script your mission statement, a formal summary of the aims and values of your company. It is a present-based statement designed to convey a sense of why your business exists to both members of the company and the external community. Answer the following questions:

1. What do we do?
2. How do we do it?
3. Whom do we do it for?
4. What value do we bring to the table?
5. Why does my business exist?

Now write your vision, a declaration of an organization's objectives, ideally based on economic foresight, intended to guide its internal decision-making. It is future-based and meant to inspire and give direction to the employees of the company, rather than to customers. Answer:

1. Where do I see my business going?
2. What does my company hope to achieve?
3. Who is my target customer base?
4. What do we want to do for them?

As of this writing, here are the influential and authoritative social media platforms that exist today. These are the platforms to which you should pay attention in creating your profile. Be aware that the internet is changing so fast today that, by the time you get your copy of this book, not all of these may be as dominant as they are now, and one or more may have been replaced. And not all of them will cater to your audience:

Twitter
Facebook
LinkedIn (professionals)

Instagram
YouTube
Yelp
Pinterest (younger crowd)
Google Hangout (already on the decline)
AVVO (lawyers only)

How to obtain the best written and video testimonials:

- Testimonials are important because people tend to follow other similarly situated people.
- A good testimonial is specific as to who wrote it and what problem the service solved for them.
- It is not vague or gushing.
- If you talk with your customers often, you'll be able to spot and extract good testimonials.
- Don't just ask for a testimonial, but walk the person through the steps required to hit the most important traits of their great testimonial.
- Never post a testimonial until you've received permission from the giver to do so.
- Among other things, ask:
    - ✓ What frustrated you before using our service?
    - ✓ Describe the moment you knew you had made the right choice with our service.
    - ✓ What did we do to prove to you that you were getting real value out of our service?

How to write a blog:

- Use keywords for search engine optimization.
- Be human. Be likeable and relatable.
- Know your audience, and appeal to them.
- Be unique. Don't just repeat what everyone else is saying.
- Ask for feedback from your readers to ascertain what content you should write.
- Answer questions readers are posting elsewhere.
- Build anticipation early so that the reader wants to keep reading.
- Link to other relevant content.
- Stay on topic.
- Blog at least once a week.
- Post the news that you have posted a new blog on all relevant discussion groups.

How to write a tweet:

- Use your 140 characters wisely.
- Keep it conversational, like you're talking to a good friend.
- Avoid business jargon.
- Be entertaining and/or informative.
- Make it shareable. It should have a purpose. It should be helpful, funny, newsworthy, or inspiring.
- Use links, pictures, videos, or quotes.
- Respond to comments.

PROFILE TIPS

- Share your personal story, including your successes, and what you have learned from your failures.
- Develop a clear message for which you are known. (A motto or a slogan can be useful in this regard.)
- Ensure that your profile reflects your mission and vision clearly.
- Spend money on a professionally created website.
- Ensure that you keep your website up-to-date.
- Set up consistent, professional profiles on your website and on all major social media platforms. Include a well-written biography, professional photos, and strategic keywords. Be meticulous. These profiles will be many people's first experience with you, and you never get a second chance to make a good first impression.
- Secure your name and business name on the major social websites. Secure the URL of your names.
- Your profile should be easy to find, both on-line and in traditional media.
- You should constantly adapt it as your career evolves and you supplement your credentials.
- Create content often. Post photos and videos. Blog at least weekly, and post to your social media sites at the same time. Tweet daily.
- Be sure that you are posting on relevant and popular platforms like LinkedIn, Facebook, Twitter, etc.
- Comment on blogs that are related to your practice area so that you position yourself correctly and come up in appropriate subject areas when people Google your name.
- Increase the number of people with whom you are connected on social media. Be a board member. Join committees and subcommittees. Speak at professional events and in panel discussions.
- Create brochures for your services. (Yes, your legal services.)
- Invest in regular training and development for yourself.
- Your profile should demonstrate your uniqueness.

- Be relatable.
- Deal with negative reviews immediately, either by politely responding or by having them removed as quickly as possible.
- Improve your SEO so that you appear on page one of relevant Google searches. Check regularly to protect that status.
- Don't forget to subtly encourage your followers to reasonable calls to action, like buying your books or attending your presentations.

PROFILE ERRORS

- Having a profile that is not conspicuous;
- Having a profile that does not accurately reflect your mission and vision;
- Not dealing with negative reviews immediately;
- Not being a member of important groups in your field;
- Failing to adapt as your career evolves; and
- Not setting yourself apart from everyone else.

Conquer Social Media Marketing

It can be daunting to establish your social media profile, especially for those of us who are less computer-savvy and who did not grow up in the era of social media. But with these tips, you'll be a pro in no time at all. Let's discuss two very different platforms, Facebook and Twitter. Just be aware that these rules should be applied to any of the constantly morphing social media platforms. Do your homework and be aware of which are prevalent; which do your client avatars frequent; on which will your prospective clients be looking for you?

Facebook

Maintain a Facebook page for your business that is public and separate from your personal page. Post consistently to this page, at least twice each day. Posts may include written posts, pictures, videos, shares, or links.

A post can focus on you, like the following: quotes, links to one of your blog posts or interviews, links to a news story about your firm, links to guest blogs or interviews that your staff has done, a discussion about an article in the news with the link to the article, etc. But some of your posts should focus on someone else, like: a blog post or article written by someone else; a news article; a book review; something that someone said that resonated with you; or an interesting or inspirational image or quote.

The purpose of posting regularly is to cultivate a community of colleagues and clients who see you as a trusted resource from whom to gain useful advice.

Even if you are linking to an article, try to grab a photo (either in the article or a related image) about 70% of the time, and post it with the article. The rest of the time, just post the link to the article.

Often, an avatar will pop up when you are linking to an article. Select an eye-catching avatar, and if one is not available, use a photo.

Tag someone or something in every post, as many as possible. This will put you on the person's or thing's wall that you are tagging and alert them that you are a fan and you are following what they are doing.

Never share something without adding a brief personal commentary, making it relevant to your brand.

When you post a new update, always "pin it to the top."

Whenever someone posts on your page wall or responds to a status update in the comments, be sure to respond every time. To successfully build your Facebook (or other social media) community, you must acknowledge those who reach out to you, even if it's just "Thanks for your insight."

TWITTER

Every day, you should perform Twitter searches directly on https://twitter.com, https://twitter.com/search-advanced, or through set up columns in Hootsuite. Pick a group of keywords or phrases that the people with whom you would like to connect, follow, or retweet, would use. If you have a blog post about a certain topic or that focuses on a certain keyword, search for that keyword. Perform the search with and without your city as the location. Review these searches daily to ascertain whether there are any people with whom you would like to connect or conversations into which you would like to insert yourself.

Additionally, review your new followers to see if there is anyone worthwhile to connect with and/or follow back. Introduce yourself to those who interest you, and mention a mutual connection or similarity. Find at least five new people to follow every week. They are often easy to find from searches.

Create Twitter lists, which will make it easier to start and inject yourself into conversations of the people who will be most valuable to you. You can make lists public or private and should use both abilities to maximize your goals. Lists could include your city, "legal news," "lawyers," etc. Spend time everyday looking through and injecting yourself into conversations of all these groups.

Find at least three new articles to tweet out each day.

Find at least five articles to retweet daily. Either retweet them straight and then send @reply to the author about the article, or mention your thought directly in the retweet. Keep in mind the lists you built above when choosing retweets.

Finally, respond to all @replies or relevant direct messages.

Natural conversation will automatically begin to develop, and you'll tend to make friends and establish "tribes" fairly quickly. Always respond to everything that is not spam.

IMPROVE YOUR PROFILE

So, you've created your pitch, you've gotten your publishing down pat, and you've begun presenting regularly. By now, as a direct result of all your hard work on the first three fortes, your profile has, by necessity, been developing itself. So why do any more work on it? Doesn't it just mature naturally?

Although developing your profile is largely about your on-line presence, a well-rounded profile also includes your off-line reputation. The best way to improve your off-line reputation is to be visible in your community. To gain free publicity, be a newsworthy story. What do you have to offer that is unique? How do you gain the attention of media professionals who can get your story out there?

There are many ways to gain media attention. The best is when you can be the first to do something noteworthy. (In my case, I put together the team of professionals that handled the first pro bono collaborative divorce in the State of Florida, and I represented the wife in that divorce.)

If you've already written a book, and thereby become an expert in your field, you will become even more newsworthy when you have your book launch. Make sure to send out press releases and post on all of the relevant on-line discussion groups, on LinkedIn, on AVVO, on Facebook, and wherever else makes sense to you. You'll be surprised who shows up for the party.

On a smaller scale, think about trying for publication in a magazine or journal. What magazines and newspapers are the people in your practice area reading? Don't contact an editor until you have sufficiently researched her publication. Once you have, e-mail her, and then follow up with a phone call. If you get a voice message, leave a brief pitch. If you reach the person, first ask if it is a good time to talk before launching into your pitch. If she is interested, immediately follow up to sustain your momentum. Be polite and diligent.

Most importantly, be a good writer. If you are concerned about your writing skills, have people whose writing skills you admire proofread your articles before you submit them.

Consider contacting your local television news stations to investigate if they have a free slot for you. News stations are often looking for informative ways to fill space, and, if you have something valuable about which you can educate the public, they will give you time to do it, often repeating the segment several times. Be sure to engage your public speaking skills; be courteous, exciting, and relevant.

Radio programs are also often looking for ways to fill their space. Some programs may even need recurring speakers. Contact your local radio stations and provide a list of possible topics on which you could speak.

Most media exposure is the result of your relationship with the journalist or producer. Research your potential journalist or producer before you contact him so that you can bond with him on a personal level. If he likes you, he is more likely to write your story or give you time on his station.

If you are struggling with your profile, consider hiring a public relations agency. Their job is to protect, enhance, or build your various reputations through the media, by analyzing your practice, finding the positive messages, and translating those messages into positive media stories. Choose the right PR practitioner who takes the time to really understand the message that you are trying to spread. Obviously, one who is passionate about your vision is even better.

The disadvantage to hiring a PR firm is the cost. But the advantages are great. You will have access to their existing media networks and relationships.

And keep in mind that you can retain their services on a short-term basis only.

Most importantly, you must be newsworthy. Remember that the journalist or producer doesn't care about you or your service. She cares about entertaining her listeners or her readers. Be sure to provide a unique, credible, and compelling perspective.

TOP TIPS FOR MARKETING ON-LINE

On-line marketing is an essential marketing tool, but, unless you hire a company to do it for you, it can be time-consuming. To make it more manageable, consider assigning various staff members each of the following sets of duties:

1. Each week, staff should search on-line for your firm's name at the following popular search engines and sites: Google, Bing, Yelp, Citysearch, and Yellowpages.com. Staff should list all the places where your firm name appears. He should ensure that the information on the website is accurate, and fix any wrong information. He should note places where the firm does not appear, but should. As with all of these tasks, he should prepare a status report each time he performs this task, and the report should be delivered to you on a day certain, every Wednesday morning, for example.

2. Staff should post daily for your firm on the following websites: Facebook, LinkedIn, Twitter, and Avvo. Concurrently, staff should prepare a report to you once each week of what was posted, for your review and 20/20 input.

3. Staff should ask current and former clients to post positive feedback on your website, LinkedIn, Facebook, Twitter, and Avvo, and should follow up on those requests until the clients either post or indicate that they would prefer not to do so. Staff should report on those reviews to you on a day certain each week. Place a tab on your website to enable clients to post testimonials themselves, with your veto power, of course.

4. Staff should regularly review the reports from your promotional channels, and then report on those reviews to you one day each week.

5. Staff should perform weekly checks regarding the number of people who clicked on your website, the number who forwarded your information, and the number of social shares. This they should also report to you on one day certain each week.

Additionally, ensure that you have a way to stay in touch with new and existing clients on your website.

Include an e-mail sign-up form on your website for potential clients who are interested in legal seminars and trainings. It should also notify you when people use it so that you can follow up.

Include a survey that clients can easily complete on your website, answering questions like whether they were happy with the results obtained and whether they would refer friends and family to the firm. Not only must you and staff then "remind" your clients that the survey exists and that you would appreciate their completion of it, but staff or you should follow up on these surveys to enforce the message that you care what your clients experience and how they perceive the services that you render them.

Entice customers to connect with you by joining your e-mail list or by interacting with you on social media. Engage regularly with them. Offer free consults, small discounts, or free books.

Offer special discounts on your website like complimentary or reduced rate supplemental services if someone refers you a client.

Always be sure to track your success so that you know what is working and what is not. Meet with a web designer regularly regarding improvements that need to be made to optimize your success.

Ask for testimonials! It is truly amazing the tributes I've received in my cases, now that I've figured out how to ask for feedback in a way that clients understand. Get them while your clients are still reeling from the success of your efforts and thus willing to do anything you ask. Explain that their feedback is crucial to getting the word out about your unique approach.

And a testimonial is the most valuable means to market your services.

The fact is that you should always debrief your clients as soon as the legal services have been rendered; I have a series of questions that helps them verbalize their thoughts, and I've been pleased by the reaffirmingly positive and specific comments my clients have made.

Ask questions like the ones in the following article. Remember that it's a conversation, so ask other questions that their answers may suggest. (Remember that it's all about active listening!) And record the conversation, if you are able, so that you can really obtain their actual words and phraseology, so necessary to convey their authenticity.

I always give them a copy when they leave, and ask them to post it (in their own words) on AVVO, on Yelp, on Google, and/or on the site of their choice, as soon as they can.

ASKING FOR TESTIMONIALS

I interview my clients at the end of every matter, and I ask very specific questions that I've designed to elicit very specific responses. I record their actual responses.

Here are some of the questions I ask:

- What was your biggest fear prior to consulting with us?
- What worked well for you?
- Did anything scare you during this matter?
- What did you like?
- What did you dislike?
- Did anything happen during your case that made you feel great?
- Did anything happen during your case that made you feel awful?
- Did you learn anything during this matter?
- Did anything surprise you during this matter?
- Do you have any critique of or compliment to your lawyer?

When I saw what kind of answers we were eliciting, I knew that I had to use these testimonials to market my practice. Although their grammar may not always perfect, former clients speak from their hearts when giving testimonials. Ask for feedback, but help your clients provide it to you. Make it easy for them by asking the right questions and recording their responses while they are still sitting in your offices. If they are not especially verbal, then rephrase and reframe. Then repeat it back to them with your suggested phraseology. Most of the time, when you ask, "Is that what you meant?" or "Did I get that right?" the answer will be "Exactly right!"

PARTNER

INTRODUCTION TO PARTNERSHIP FORTES

Partnerships are important in all businesses. Let's face it; none of us is exceptional at everything. Partnerships offer you the opportunity to do what you are really good at, the things that you (hopefully) enjoy doing, while your partner performs the tasks in which he excels and at which you may not be as skilled. In partnering, you can create an exceptional team of people, using each person's most outstanding talents. Also, you will expand your pool of contacts because your partner's contact becomes your contact.

In this section, you will learn tips on how to form a partnership and with whom to partner. You'll learn how to maintain your already established partnerships. You'll learn how to get the most from your partnerships.

I'll also discuss errors to avoid when partnering.

PARTNERSHIP BASICS

Form strategic alliances with referral sources and with other influencers.

Types of partnerships that business people (not necessarily lawyers) can enjoy (other than business partnerships composed of lawyers who have entered into a formal partnership relationship with each other):

- *Affiliate* partners are paid a commission to recommend your services.
- *Brand* partners make you look good, like a celebrity endorsement.
- *Operational* partners assist you to deliver a better service to more people by helping to perform the work that you cannot do on your own. Often, this will include your own team partners, please who work with you or for you in your law firm.
- *Product* partners supply you with additional products that add value to your business. They increase your capacity to deliver value and solve problems for your clients.
- *Financial* partners provide the financial resources to scale your enterprise.
- *Sponsorship* partners provide funding or other resources to support your not-for-profit and/or teaching endeavors.
- *Mission* partners work to help you further your mission, usually because their mission is either the same as or aligned with yours (and can also be sponsorship partners).

Form relationships with already active referral partners:

- Your relatives;
- Your friends and neighbors;
- Your employees;
- Other lawyers; and
- Former clients.

Develop relationships with potential referral partners:

- Always have your business cards handy to pass out, whether you are at a professional luncheon or a sports event.
- When you receive a business card, immediately follow up and set up a

lunch or something similar with the person whose card you have.

- Ask your current clients for referrals. Offer a discount or credit if your client refers a new client to you, or send a gift. At the very least, send a handwritten thank-you card; so few people do these days, that that gesture really stands out.
- Look for professionals on-line, especially through LinkedIn, and reach out to them.
- Stand out from the crowd so that others want to partner with you.
- Be clear to your referral network about who your ideal client is.

Support your ongoing relationships with these referral partners:

- Actively refer your clients to other appropriate service providers.
- Nurture your relationships with your partners by getting to know them on a more personal level. Take them to lunch. Show interest in them and in the work that they do.
- Do a good job and be friendly so that people want to refer potential clients to you.
- Seek partnerships with people who work in fields that complement the services that you provide to your clients.
- Show your appreciation when a partner refers a new client to you. Send a thank-you note. Take the partner out to lunch.

PARTNERSHIP TIPS

- Access people with the skills, talents, and resources that you need for your law business to succeed but for which your time would be more wisely spent elsewhere.
- Ask for referrals, especially right after someone has complimented your work.
- Recommend and resell other people's products and services, and encourage those businesses to do the same for you.
- If you realize that someone in your referral network is not performing at your level, disassociate from them so that your reputation isn't impacted.
- Be the type of person and run the type of law business to which you would want to refer others.
- Get endorsed by a bigger brand than yours.
- Foster a spirit of partnership in your team by treating your employees and others around you with the same level of respect that you would treat a business partner.

PARTNERSHIP ERRORS

- Not actively pursuing referral partnerships;

- Being rude. You never know to whom you're talking and the connections he may have;
- Doing a bad job;
- Not showing appreciation for referrals; and
- Not honing all of your five marketing fortes, from *Pitch* to *Publish*, from *Present* to *Profile*, all the way through to *Partnership*.

One must focus on strengthening all of these marketing faculties, your fortes, in order; one feeds into the next. Until you are able to confidently and effectively pitch, you won't know your subject matter well enough to publish regularly about it. Publishing often increases your knowledge and memory of a subject, making you a better presenter. Presenting will improve your profile, and when you have an impressive profile, more remarkable colleagues will want to partner with you.

Ask anyone who might be right for you to partner with for her story. Listen actively and with your inner hearing triggered, as well. You never know how you'll find your next partner, or who that will be. I'm constantly fascinated by the unusual stories people will tell me about their childhoods, their sweethearts, their college experiences, their customers and clients, their own children, their hobbies. . . . I could go on and on.

Here's my story. What's yours?

Unique

When I was a little girl, my best friend, who lived two doors down, was named Robin Robinson. We were born on the very same day in 1957. We lived on Galway Circle, and we attended school at Robinwood Elementary. (Poor Robin; the kids picked on her mercilessly.)

There came a time when Robin's mother placed her in the neighborhood Brownies troop. And, because Robin was in Girl Scouts, I wanted to be in a Girl Scout troop, as well.

"Mom, can I be a Brownie?"

"Sure, honey. I don't see why not."

A few days passed, and no mention of Girl Scouts. Robin was going to her meeting right after school.

When I arrived home, I asked, "Mom, am I going to Brownies?"

"Oh, Honey! I'm so sorry. I checked into that for you, but the answer is no."

"Why not?" I asked perplexed.

"Because we're Jewish," my mother explained.

In retrospect, this was really no explanation at all, but I was too young to follow through with the obvious inquiry.

"Oh," was all I said. I hadn't even known that we were Jewish. Clearly, that made me different from the rest of the little girls.

The next year, I was halfway through second grade when the school promoted me into the third grade. I left Robin behind and our friendship evaporated into thin air. I was lonely as the only second grader in the third grade, but I had little time to feel sorry for myself; I was too busy trying to keep up with the rest of my class.

That was also the year that my parents divorced, and my mother relocated us 3000 miles away. With no other recourse, we moved in with my grandparents.

New school. I was lonely again as the only new kid in class, but the "newness" soon wore off. It was quickly replaced with a different kind of "different" when the other kids discovered that I was a year younger than everyone else. And that I still managed to excel in my reading and on all my tests.

That was the year that I began to develop a competitive streak.

That was also the year that my mother explained that, although my father was Christian, she was not. Now that we were back in her hometown, she enrolled all four of us kids in the local synagogue, where she herself had attended religious school as a child.

When I was in the seventh grade, I discovered that my friends, who were all boys, had all started attending *bar mitzvah* classes at our synagogue, Tuesdays and Thursdays after "regular school." I understood the classes to be an extension of the Sunday School that we all, both girls and boys, attended on Saturday mornings.

Soon after classes had begun the next Saturday morning, I ventured down the hallway to our rabbi's office and poked my head in. (He had no secretary to guard his door.)

"Come on in, Joryn. What can I do for you this morning?" Although he was obviously in the middle of preparing his sermon, his eyes crinkled a welcome in his seamed face.

"Well, two things, Rabbi Shankman." I backed up to and, grabbing the arms of the overstuffed chair in front of his desk, pushed myself up into it. My toes barely touched the floor. "I would like to know if Temple Israel is planning to offer conversational Hebrew lessons this year. I would really love to learn Hebrew. And can I enroll in the *bar mitzvah* classes with the boys?"

In retrospect, I know that the rabbi was always tickled that I liked to excel. Thus, Rabbi Shankman and I struck a deal; G'veret Kalb would offer conversational Hebrew one hour prior to the Tuesday/Thursday *bar mitzvah* classes, which she also taught, and I could attend classes with the boys afterwards, despite that my synagogue did not "*bar mitzvah*" the girls.

No one else enrolled in the conversational Hebrew classes. I attended these classes all by myself for two years. And, for over a year, I attended the *bar mitzvah* classes with the boys, as the lone little girl.

The idea of being unique, of being different from those around me, grew on me. You could say that I made lemonade from the lemons that the Girl Scouts had handed me when I was seven. When I graduated law school at 23 years old, this translated into my primary objective in practicing law, to "make new law." I would take those difficult cases that no one else wanted, in which there was an opportunity to "make a difference," to "change the world," by making new law. I was especially interested in convincing an appellate court to overrule a statute, strike down a regulation, write an opinion that had never been written before, etc. On one occasion, I convinced the Supreme Court of Florida to strike down a statute that, I argued and the justices agreed, violated the state constitution.

What is it about you that attracts you to your mission? Do you share that with others? Is it part of your pitch? Is it one of the stories that you tell to move people to action? Share your story with me at Joryn@OpenPalmLaw.com; I'll be interested to hear it.

Build Your Referral Network

To be successful in any business, you must have a strong network of referral sources. So how do you develop and maintain such relationships?

First, join two to three diverse organizations, whether social, cultural, political, religious, charitable, professional, or of some other genre. Sign up with a general business group, as well as, perhaps, a club related to a hobby that you enjoy. You will thus enjoy a diverse group of connections who can provide valuable contacts.

Now, get involved. One of the easiest ways to build your network is to establish trust by showing interest in others and by spending time making your own contribution to your community.

On the other hand, don't spread yourself too thin. It is better to be choosy about which organizations you join and to give each of those you do join your full attention.

Also, while it's easy to get stuck in a rut and to remain involved with organizations with which you have been active for years, or to join only groups composed of other professionals with whom you already have relationships, try to branch out; join groups outside of your comfort zone.

Next, refer to others. This will sound crass, but I don't mean it to be, and it is absolutely true; when you know that someone likes you, it feels good, and you tend to like that person more because of it. The same goes for referrals. When someone refers to you, you are more likely to refer to that referral source, and vice versa.

Furthermore, if you speak well of others whom you admire, they are more likely to speak highly of you. And the more good that is said of you, the more people will want to retain your services. So, speak well of those whom you admire, and what goes around should come back around.

Connect with possible referral sources on a personal level. Once someone considers you his friend, he will want you to succeed and will be more willing to help you in your endeavors.

You should also showcase your expertise by offering free lectures or by writing articles for local publications. Always include your contact information at the end of your lecture or article. And, as always, consider whether a call to action is appropriate.

Use digital marketing to make even more connections. Run searches on yourself to ensure that you have a good on-line reputation. If you don't, fix it. If you do, improve it. Write blogs, update profiles, and post often. Most clients conduct on-line research to ascertain professionals who might be able to assist with their problem and to check the reputations of those professionals whom they consider retaining.

Don't be ashamed to ask for a referral. Never miss an opportunity to provide your call to action. That being said, nobody likes someone whom he or she feels is constantly trying to get something out of him or her. So, avoid being too pushy or asking for a referral at inappropriate times.

And let's not forget the most invaluable referral source of all. Do an exceptional job for your current clients. This requires providing superior service, excellent communication, and true value to your clients. By just being good at what you do, people will refer clients to you. Don't forget the power of your reputation.

And do not neglect to ask referral partners who thank you for taking good care of their referrals and for doing such good work for them to also give you an endorsement. Client testimonials are not the only testimonials out there. Professional endorsements can be just as valuable in helping you obtain new referral partners.

Treat your current clients as the valuable commodities that they are. Foster your relationships with them. Remind them that you appreciate their referrals. Offer them a reward for referrals.

Don't forget that once you have established your network, it is important to maintain communication with them and to provide value to your referral network. Remain visible to them so that they don't forget about you. Continue participating in your organizations. Continue giving lectures. Invite your referral sources to lunch or coffee or wine once in a while. Send thank-you notes when you receive a referral. Refer back when appropriate. Send holiday cards or throw small holiday parties. Build personal relationships with your referral sources. Don't let your referral sources forget just how wonderful you are!

TIPS FOR PITCHING A POTENTIAL PARTNER

When I say "investors," I use the term loosely to refer to anyone who might be interested in "investing" in my mission, whether it's a potential business partner that I'm pitching to sponsor my trainings or my speakers' bureau, a potential referral partner such as a legal services organization that can send me clients for my pro bono project, possible associates or partners in my law firm, or likely committee volunteers to work on organizing a conference. While pitching to a potential partner is fairly similar to the other types of pitching we've discussed, there are some differences.

1. Practicing your partner pitch is even more important because you are more likely to be nervous when pitching to a potential partner. Practice it daily. Know it by heart. Give your pitch to friends and family, and have them critique you. Listen to their comments, and use them to improve your pitch.

2. Keep it simple. You may feel inclined to slip into jargon and legalese in an effort to impress your potential partner or because he is likely a bit savvier than the average layperson to whom you usually pitch. But, regardless of his education level, keep in mind his likely knowledge of your particular interest, so explain it in a way that he will understand. After all, if you make him feel stupid, he won't want to partner with or invest in you, or otherwise help you.

3. Before anything else, explain what you are offering him. What is the benefit to him of partnering with you? Why should he be interested? Then, too, be ready to explain what the benefit to *you* is, so that he understands the powerful give-and-take you propose.

4. Understand that his time is valuable. Most professionals have busy schedules. Be sure to arrive early, and keep your pitch to the time allotted. Most partnership pitches last only ten minutes, unless this is a one-to-one or he approached *you*. (Think of *Shark Tank*.) If you present a PowerPoint, limit it to eight to ten slides. (See Appendix 13 for an example of a brief PowerPoint.)

5. Be prepared for the professional or investor to interrupt you with questions. Prepare responses to probable questions beforehand. Keep them brief, yet explanatory. Ensure that you answer the exact question that he asks. (Again, think of *Shark Tank*.)

6. Read his cues. If he appears anxious, bored, or confused, respond appropriately by wrapping up your pitch or explaining confusing concepts.

7. Have a project, business, team, partnership, sponsorship, or committee plan ready to hand him. Your partner is not likely to remember everything that you said in your pitch, so you must provide him with a takeaway. Also, he is more likely to remember you if you appeal not only to his sense of sound during your pitch, but also to his senses of sight and touch by giving him a document to peruse later. (And, by the way, your plan should be more specific than your pitch and should offer details that back up any claims that you may have made.)

8. As with any pitch, begin with a brief introduction of who you are and what you do. Start strong by beginning with a compelling story or a thought-provoking statistic. Define the problem that you solve. Keep it concise and easy for the partner to explain to others, just in case the decision isn't solely up to him. (You may not realize that he has shadow consultants, like a husband or a wife, at the very least.) Explain your solution and why it is important to you. Establish credibility by offering examples of what others say about you. Impress partners with what you and your team have accomplished to date. Describe the members on your team and how each is valuable. If an investor, include an exit strategy that explains how he will make a significant profit or achieve a specific benefit within three to seven years, or achieve a certain committee goal, and then move on.

9. In addition to the contents of a regular pitch, your partnership pitch should include some additional information:

    a. Include a realistic target market.
    b. Discuss how you will reach your customers and how much that will cost.
    c. Explain how you are different from your competitors.
    d. Be specific about how your project, business, team, project, training, or committee concept will spread the word, make money, attract clients, or otherwise accomplish your goal or forward your mission.
    e. If relevant, explain your financial projections over the next three to five years. Make sure your numbers make sense and your calculations are accurate. Your partners or investors will check, probably on their smart phones, as you are talking.
    f. Clearly spell out your funding needs, if there are any, or your

staffing requirements. Include how much money or staffing you need, why you need it, for what it will be used, and the intended outcome.

10. Ask your partners or investors to sign a non-disclosure agreement. Have one handy to provide to him on the spot.

11. Wait for him to begin the discussion of valuation and pricing with a term sheet. Pushing him too early will likely get you nowhere fast.

12. Learn from the constructive criticism of your potential partners. Don't take it personally. Even if they turn you down, their advice may land you the deal with the next partner.

Follow these tips, and you may soon have the funding or the partnership you need to begin your dream project.

Partnership Dysfunctions

Although we never refer to them this way, our staff members are our teammates or our partners in the practice of law. And the smaller the law firm, the more critical the role of each staff member becomes. So those of us with small law offices especially must be aware of common partnership dysfunctions and how to avoid them.

Partnerships that work as teams can make magic happen because a group effort can enhance the work of an individual. However, it is not guaranteed that the efforts of a group will be better than the efforts of an individual. There are some common dysfunctions of a team that should be avoided, or at least mitigated. These dysfunctions are:

1. Lack of bounds;
2. Feeling that new members are always needed;
3. Feeling that bigger is better;
4. Lack of a compelling direction;
5. Lack of enabling structures;
6. Absence of trust;
7. Inattention to results;
8. Fear of conflict and tension;
9. Lack of commitment and failure to buy into decisions; and
10. Avoidance of accountability.

A lack of clarity and bounds regarding who is on the team can make a team less effective than it might otherwise be. Not everyone will be a good fit for the team. In order to avoid this hazard, leaders and partners should make hard decisions as to who should be on the team. Some feelings might get hurt, but a leader should look at what is best for the group effort.

Feeling that you always need to enlist new members is another pitfall of teamwork. It is a fallacy to think that teams become so comfortable that performance falls off. Rather, through experience, team members learn to operate as partners. A team that has gelled should be allowed to work together in future endeavors. That being said, the team should be open to inviting new members when it would benefit the team.

Bigger is not necessarily better when it comes to teams. Bigger teams can make work unwieldy, dragging out the time it takes to complete it. It can also make it difficult to come to consensus. So, weigh the benefits of adding a team member with unique skills and qualities against the drawbacks of creating too large a working group.

A lack of a compelling direction is detrimental to teams. In order for teams to remain focused, a leader should clearly articulate the goal and direction toward which the team is working. In addition, the steps to achieving each goal should be small so that the team feels that it is making progress at any given moment.

Besides a lack of compelling direction, a lack of enabling structures can be detrimental to teams. Leaders should provide and make explicit the norms of conduct expected in the group. Active listening; using a respectful tone of voice; not interrupting others while they are speaking, etc., are such norms.

Teamwork can suffer from a lack of trust, i.e. the failure on the part of team members to understand and open up to one another. In order to avoid this pitfall, encourage your team members to socialize with each other. Because team members should be encouraged to trust one another, they should be willing to admit their mistakes, weaknesses, and concerns. Team members can often open up about their personal lives before they can offer trust in their professional endeavors.

They can also take the Myers-Briggs Type Indicator. Paying attention to personality types can enable team members to cater to each other's personality needs, allowing them to partner more capably with each other.

Inattention to results is a dysfunction that can be caused by team members seeking out individual recognition and attention at the expense of collective results. However, no matter how good an individual on the team might be feeling about his individual/personal situation, if the team loses, everyone loses.

To counter this danger, make the results that you should achieve so clear to everyone that no one would ever consider doing something purely to enhance his individual status or ego. Define goals and results in a way that is simple enough to grasp easily, and specific enough to be actionable.

Fear of conflict and tension is another trap for teams. Teammates should feel free to go out on a limb and take risks in order to engage in open, constructive dialogue. Out-of-the-box thinkers should be allowed to voice their disruptive opinions and spark others' thinking. However, watch out that you don't create an artificial sense of harmony.

Lack of commitment and failure to buy into decisions also makes teams less effective. Allowing people to weigh in so that they feel heard can alleviate any lack of commitment. This is why debriefing after accomplishing each goal is so important.

Finally, a lack of accountability can stymie a team. We should hold each other accountable for high standards of behavior and performance. Break a group goal into small, manageable tasks and assign each task to a particular individual so that it is clear who is responsible. Then have regular meetings for updates. This keeps people from feeling that others are not doing their part. Each person has clearly defined duties, and, if someone is not carrying his load, it will be clear who that is, to both him and his teammates.

Also, team members will want to avoid looking like slackers, so they will be more likely to complete the tasks for which they are responsible.

Teamwork can make magic happen. All it takes to see the magic of a group is a little attention to prevent certain dysfunctions from happening.

No A**holes Allowed

Assholes . . . we all know one. At least one. Each of us may act like one, once in a blue moon. Unfortunately, there are situations in which being an asshole can help you.

Before I go on, let me apologize. I searched for a less vulgar synonym for the word I use above, and was unable to find any substitute even remotely as descriptively pejorative. "Jerk" doesn't carry the same impact; jerks can be nice. "Bastard" doesn't fit the bill; it's simply not detestable enough. "Shithead" falls short; such a person is not as contemptible. And "ass" alone is used too often in an affectionate manner; "asshole" never is. So, forgive me for using such a rude term throughout this analysis, but I had no choice.

Now, let me explain my initial announcement. I was retained by a doctor who had been involved in an ugly custody battle prior to his final divorce hearing. But even after the final judgment was entered, his mentally ill ex-wife continued making unfounded allegations against him of sexual abuse against their small daughter and physical abuse against her, constantly involving the police, *Children and Family Services*, and the court system. This seemingly endless litigation was costly and stressful and tiring for many reasons before the ex retained her ninth attorney, the . . . a--hole. He was just the icing on the cake.

This guy was so despicable that he himself bragged to us, early on, that one of his own clients had shot him! He made my life and my client's and staff's lives miserable. He verbally attacked everyone in the room (except his client) during depositions, phone calls, and pretty much every interaction. His cockiness, his rudeness, his slurs, and his low blows made us dread every encounter. For months, he cast a dark cloud over my entire team as we waited for his next offense or insult. Even my regular court reporter found this guy contemptible, despite that he (said that he) liked her, after I introduced them at my first hearing with him, and he used her for any depositions he scheduled in the case after that.

Sadly, his destructive attitude worked. My already beaten-down client, despite having won repeatedly in court up until then, was so intimidated that he would have agreed to almost anything, just to end the litigation. When it was finally over, I vowed never to work with such an a--hole again, if I could help it.

In *The No Asshole Rule*, Robert I. Sutton explains how to build a civilized workplace environment free of negative employees who seek to destroy (or at least make miserable) their co-workers.[5] Sutton describes two tests to determine whether a person is an a--hole:

---

[5] Robert I. Sutton, PhD, *The No Asshole Rule* (New York, 2007).

> Test One: After talking to the alleged a--hole, does the "target" feel oppressed, humiliated, de-energized, or belittled by the person. In particular, does the target feel worse about him- or herself?
>
> Test Two: Does the alleged a--hole aim his or her venom at people who are less powerful rather than at those who are more powerful?

Sutton lists 12 common everyday actions of a--holes:

1. Personal insults;
2. Invasion of one's "personal territory;"
3. Uninvited physical contact;
4. Threats and intimidation;
5. Sarcastic "jokes" and "teasing;"
6. Withering e-mails;
7. Status slaps intended to humiliate their victims;
8. Public shaming;
9. Rude interruptions;
10. Two-faced attacks;
11. Dirty looks; and
12. Treating people as if they are invisible.

Sutton also differentiates between temporary a--holes and certified a--holes. Thus, anyone can have a bad day, but you should avoid working with certified a--holes.

The attorney I describe above was, without a doubt, a certified a--hole. He demonstrated despicable qualities in every interpersonal interaction. I always felt worse about myself after dealing with him. And while he never displayed his appalling behavior to the judge, a person with more power, he was even more offensive to my staff, those with less. Sutton emphasizes that "the difference between how a person treats the powerless versus the powerful" is a good determiner of human character.

So why bring this up in *Partnership*? Sutton points out that "negative interactions [have] a fivefold stronger effect on mood than positive interactions." Nobody wants to work on a team whose members are always in a bad mood. It is difficult to be creative and productive when you are on edge, anticipating your next rude encounter.

Further, such people can be costly. How?

- They distract team members from their tasks because the victims spend more time dodging from and coping with nasty encounters than on the job at hand.
- A--holes deplete creativity because victims are less likely to take risks or to brainstorm for fear of how the a--hole will react. Victims

lose motivation.
- Time is wasted disciplining a--holes and calming victims.
- Finally, victims become ill from stress and are more likely to be absent.

So how do you enforce the "no assholes allowed" rule?

- Don't hire them.
- Don't team with them.
- Don't partner with them on committees, at work, in business, on projects, or otherwise,
- If they are already work with you, don't let them recruit others.
- Get rid of a--holes fast. While everyone can have a bad day, if you realize that someone is a recurrent, certified a--hole, remove him from your organization, your project, your committee, or your law firm.

But if you do include such a person in your organization:

- Be sure that the group understands that he is an example of bad behavior.
- Treat a--holes as they should be treated.
- Don't condone their behavior.
- Don't give them too much power.
- Don't let a--holes run your organizations.

Don't let one bad apple spoil the bunch. Employ the "no assholes allowed" rule.

CREATING A MARKETING PLAN

It's important to actually prepare and then perform your marketing plan. Recall that there are five fortes of effective marketing: attaining your clarity (I call it *Pitch*), establishing your credibility (*Publish*), achieving your coherence (*Present*), becoming conspicuous (*Profile*), and enabling your connectivity (*Partner*). You should have realized by now that, although they do build one on the next, you don't complete one before starting the next.

Instead, start by creating a task list. Outline your next year of marketing effort now; summarize what you plan to do, beginning now and ending a year from now. Make a list of all of the tasks laid out in the various forte basics and tips; attach a completion deadline to each and then get to work.

I'll give you your first four weeks here and you can take it from there. Be sure to attach completion deadlines to each of these, recognizing that some of these tasks you will repeat weekly or monthly, as necessary and as I've suggested below.

Week One

1. Read *Introduction* (page 1) and the *Marketing* section, commencing on page 3 of *From Rookie to Rainmaker, How to Grow Your Law Business* (hereinafter *Rainmaker).*
2. Read *Pitch,* pages 27-41 of *Rainmaker.*
3. Create your quick pitch on this, Day One. That same day:
    a. Type your quick pitch in font large enough to read from a distance.
    b. Print several copies.
    c. Post it on the fridge, on the bathroom mirror, and at your desk. Put a copy on the passenger seat of your car, so that it's handy at stoplights.
    d. Practice your pitch three times before leaving your home each day, this week and every week.
    e. Practice your pitch three times on your way to work each day.
    f. Deliver your pitch to at least three people each day. Gauge the results and begin fine tuning the words in your pitch and your emphasis on them.

    Do not wait to do these tasks until you are sure your pitch is finalized. If you do that, it will never be final. Do these tasks starting the first day. Start pitching the first day.
4. As you fine tune your pitch, retype it and repost it every time in all the same places as before.
5. Review your contacts; list all referral sources that you already know, and any that occur to you on this first go-round. (Clean up your contact database while you're at

it.)

6. Also read *Partnership Basics*, starting at page 137, and *Build Your Referral Network*, beginning at page 143.
7. Schedule one-to-ones with your existing referral sources. These can be lunch meetings, or coffee or breakfast meetings. Perhaps a glass of wine works best for both of you. In any event, these are opportunities at which you can get to know each other, and each other's businesses, better. At those meetings, deliver your pitch so that they can see your passion and so that you can hone your pitch.
8. Consider whom you can refer to *your* referral sources. Develop the habit of referring at least one person daily. Remember that people refer to people who refer to them. Be one of those people doing the referring; only then can you expect to receive referrals.

Week Two

1. Apply to join a referral-networking group. BNI is one such organization. Google "BNI (your city)" and find a list of area chapters with the list of professions already filled. This will let you know which chapter has the seat that is appropriate for you open. If not BNI, research some other networking groups in your locale and pursue a seat in one of them.
2. List the people you know in the media.
    a. Consider radio, TV, podcast, newspapers, magazines, and any other media that comes to mind.
    b. Contact each media person you know and schedule a one-to-one meeting to chat about his work and your efforts to market your practice.
    c. Send an idea to be on a show or to be interviewed.
    d. Arrange to appear on the show.
    e. Prepare the interview questions and your suggested responses for your appearance and provide those to the relevant media person ahead of time.

Week Three

1. Read *Publish*, at pages 55-91 of *Rainmaker*. See especially the tips in *Publishing Basics*, starting on page 59.
2. Construct the avatar of your perfect reader. What is the burning question that your avatar wants answered?
3. Re-read *Find the Right Publications*, page 67 of *Rainmaker.*
4. Review publications from all organizations to which you belong or which are pertinent to your work (newsletters, magazines, e-zines, etc.). Which of these might be a good publication for you?
5. Contact the publications' committees and editorial boards to determine how articles are submitted and what the requirements are for those articles.
6. Create a list of legal topics on which you are knowledgeable and stories you want to tell.
7. Outline and prepare your first article for submission.

8. Re-read *Write Must-Follow Blogs*, page 87 of *Rainmaker.*
9. Write and post your first blog. It should be 500-2000 words.
10. Set up a Word file that holds all of your draft blogs and articles. (You can work on these at your leisure, if you aren't able to finalize them when you first write them.)
11. Set up another Word file for final blogs and articles. (You will repurpose these later on.)
12. Set up a section on your website to archive all posted blogs and published articles.
13. Submit your first article and post it to your website when it's published.

Week Four

1. Write and post your second blog. It should be 500-2000 words. Load the final version into your Word file that holds all final drafts of blogs and articles. Continue doing this weekly.
2. Re-read *Write Compelling Tweets*, at page 89, *Rainmaker.*
3. Begin tweeting the news that you are blogging, and use quotes from your first two blogs to drive traffic to your blogs from Twitter. Continue doing this with every subsequent blog that you write.
4. Read *Profile*, pages 117-125, *Rainmaker.*
5. Research existing discussion groups on Facebook and LinkedIn and join the ones you like.
6. Post your first two blogs to the discussion groups to which they are relevant. Continue doing this with every subsequent blog that you write.
7. Create a file on your Internet Explorer program where you can save all discussion groups you have joined for quick access later, when you post your next blogs.
8. Start asking and answering questions on the discussion groups you have joined on Facebook and LinkedIn. This will raise your profile.
9. Pay attention to any comments posted on your own blogs and be sure to respond to all of them, even if only to thank the writer for commenting!
10. Review your first four weeks; acknowledge your accomplishments and commit to completing any item missed or incomplete before the week is over.

Congratulations! You've completed your first four weeks!

Repeating tasks:

Weekly:

Update your list of legal topics (Week 3, step 6, above).
Review and revise, if necessary, your elevator pitch.
Review and revise, if necessary, your social pitch.

Monthly:

Choose and purchase one of the books in Appendix 8 on pages 185-187. Read it.

Review and revise your FB and LI profiles.

Appendices

APPENDIX 1
SAMPLE SELF PROFILE

- *Goals - 2017*
  - 6/1/17 Publish *From Lawyer to Law Firm, Champions, and Puzzle*
  - 9/30/17 Establish *Open Palm Collaborative Conflict Resolution*
  - 12/31/17 Publish five *OPPress* books
  - 12/31/17 Grow *OPLaw* to five lawyers
  - 12/31/18 Open the *First Peace Center*

- *Accomplishments*
  - Fastest guilty verdict in the county
  - Fastest appellate reversal in 2nd DCA
  - Made new law 15 times in 33 years
  - Received 16th *A. Sherman Christensen Award* in the U.S. Supreme Court
  - Published five collaborative law books
  - Served 10 years as editor-in-chief of *The Federal Lawyer* national magazine
  - Won Federal Bar's *President's Award*
  - Launched *Cheatwood American Inn of Court* (a platinum inn) 29 years ago
  - Founded *Coordinating Council of Florida Inns*
  - Facilitated establishment of 40+ inns
  - Published A *Stepmother's Cookbook*
  - Authored *Florida Civil Motions Practice*
  - Appointed *Stetson University* Professor of Law
  - Served as Lead Articles Editor, *The Tax Lawyer,* an ABA law review
  - Worked as a US Steelworker
  - Founded/captained *Yale* Women's Varsity Soccer
  - Graduated *Yale* at 19 years old
  - Accepted by *Yale* without a high school diploma

- *Referrals – People who want to:*
  - Restructure a relationship (partnership, romantic, employment...), not destroy it
  - Maintain privacy
  - Maintain confidentiality
  - Minimize cost resolving dispute
  - Minimize time resolving dispute
  - Minimize damage to others
  - Avoid putting kids, friends, employees & clients "in middle"

- *Referral Sources*
  - Marriage & family counselors
  - Religious & pastoral counselors
  - Business partners or employees
  - Financial consultants
  - Health & wellness providers Parents & other family members
  - Day care providers
  - Friends: friends don't let friends suffer through a conventional divorce court war; they help them resolve their disputes with dignity, peacefully & respectfully

- *Passions*
  - *Changing the Way the World Resolves Conflict®*
  - Restructuring and Healing Families
  - Collaborative & Courtless Practice
  - Training Lawyers
  - Writing & Reading

Appendix 2
Sample Firm Brochure

This is an 8x8 tri-fold that I created for my law practice. It is a single long sheet of heavy paper, folded twice. The first set of panels is the "outside" three, with the far right folding on top, the middle panel being the back side of the brochure, and the far-left testimonials page folding inside.

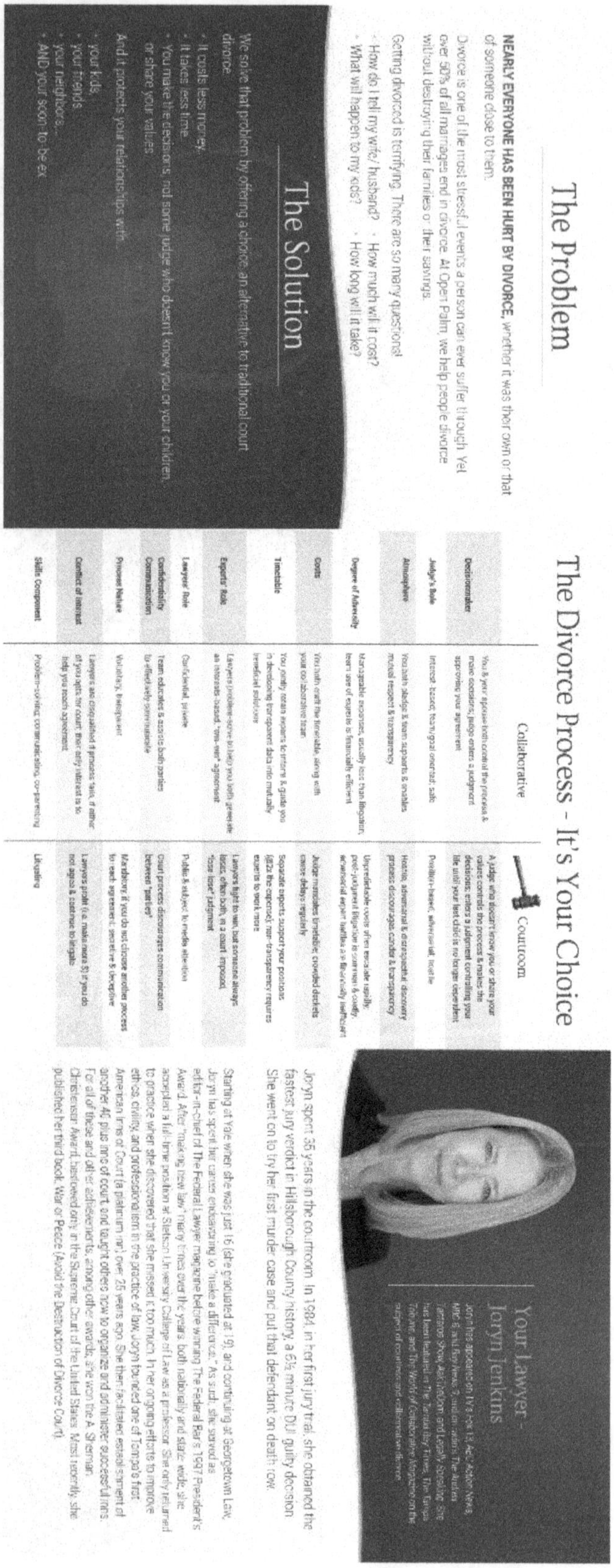

The second set of three panels is the inside; if you simply opened the brochure and laid it out in front of you, this is what you would see inside.

Appendix 3
Sample Media Release

I irrevocably give permission and consent to Joryn Jenkins and Open Palm, and any media outlet or source to whom this may be assigned by Joryn Jenkins and Open Palm, to use any and all facets of my collaborative practice story(ies) shared with Joryn Jenkins and/or Open Palm, or its agent, employee, or designee, as well as my photograph, name, likeness, interview, audio and/or video recording, information, and/or comments regarding that story or stories, recorded in any way or format whatsoever, in any and all of Joryn Jenkins' efforts to publicize interdisciplinary collaborative divorce, in general, and the story of the collaborative dissolution of marriage that I shared with her and/or Open Palm, in particular.

I understand and agree that my information, photograph, name, likeness, interview, audio and/or video recording, and/or comments may be placed on websites, magazines, newspapers, television newscasts, and/or other media outlets, as well as in books and/or other published works about interdisciplinary collaborative divorce.

By signing this release, I relinquish monetary claims and any and all rights to publicity, and agree to hold Joryn Jenkins and Open Palm harmless for any liability arising from participation in efforts to publicize interdisciplinary collaborative practice. I state that I have no conflict of interest with the subject matter and that I enter into this agreement of my own free will.

_____________________________ _____________________________

Signature Date

____

Print Name

_____________________________ _____________________________

Witness 1 Signature Witness 1 Print Name

_____________________________ _____________________________

Witness 2 Signature Witness 2 Print Name

Appendix 4
Sample Press Release

For Immediate Release

Tampa, Florida/ May 11, 2015 – **Open Palm Law** has won the 2015 *Outstanding Pro Bono Service by a Law Firm Award* given by the Thirteenth Judicial Circuit. Since January 1, 2014, Open Palm Law has contributed a total of 448.30 hours of pro bono work.

In June 2012, the firm's founder, Joryn Jenkins, initiated a *Pro Bono Project* for the Collaborative Divorce Institute of Tampa Bay, which later became *Next Generation Divorce* Practice Group. This project offers divorce services for free to qualified clients who might otherwise be unaware of this courtless, less stressful alternative to traditional courtroom divorce. As organizer and chair of the *Pro Bono Project*, Ms. Jenkins has worked diligently to encourage other professionals in the collaborative community (lawyers, mental health professionals, and financial specialists) to accept *pro bono* collaborative cases. Joryn has spent numerous hours reviewing possible cases, working with Bay Area Legal Services and other organizations that offer *pro bono* divorce services to bring their staffs up to speed on collaborative practice, speaking to groups of other professionals to get them involved and excited about assisting lower income clients with their collaborative divorces, and then mentoring those professionals who do volunteer their time.

Joryn is also producing a collaborative divorce *pro bono* project handbook, not just to be used locally, but to share across the state and the nation. Because of Joryn's efforts, Tampa Bay leads the nation in its efforts to offer *pro bono* collaborative divorce services and provides a model for fledgling *pro bono* collaborative divorce programs everywhere.

In 2013, Ms. Jenkins obtained the referral of, conducted the intake for, and represented one of the parties in the first *pro bono* collaborative dissolution of marriage case in Florida. Since then, she has handled many *pro bono* collaborative divorces. The *Pro Bono Project* focuses on Hillsborough, Pinellas, Manatee, Pasco, and Sarasota Counties.

About Open Palm

The lawyers at Open Palm are driven to inspire confidence in the law and the legal profession by rendering the highest quality of legal services, and by demonstrating ethics, creativity, and caring in the practice of law.

Media Contact
Joryn Jenkins
813-870-3839
Website: http://www.OpenPalmLaw.com/
E-mail: Joryn@OpenPalmLaw.com
# # #

Appendix 5
Sample Press Interview Outline

Who is Joryn Jenkins?

I'm an attorney who's been trying cases for 37 years. Over the years, I've seen how divorce court can ruin people, not just financially, but also emotionally. When I learned about collaborative law, I just knew that this was the right thing, and I wanted to be a part of it. The sign in front of my building used to say "Joryn Jenkins & Associates, Trial Attorneys." Now it says "Open Palm Law."

So, what exactly is Collaborative Law?

It's a process for resolving disputes without going to court. Each party retains his own lawyer. The lawyers get together and hire a facilitator (or coach) and a financial person, both also collaboratively-trained. Everyone on the team agrees to the ground rules, which include that they will settle the issues privately, without resort to court.

The average divorce will bankrupt most people and causes hatred that lasts forever. The Open Palm Divorce is private, cheaper, quicker, safer, less stressful, and less likely to cause hard feelings. We call it the kinder, gentler divorce. Simply put, the husband and wife, and their lawyers, work together without going to court. They hire "middlemen," who help the process. If it all works out, then the divorce is accomplished quickly and easily, and saves everyone money and grief.

How does it work?

Collaborative divorce takes place over a series of meetings, as many as are necessary:

- Between each client and each neutral professional;
- Between each client and his or her lawyer; and
- Of the full team of clients and professionals.

No judge; no court. This is the heart of the Open Palm Divorce: if the parties throw in the towel and file in court, their lawyers are off the case. The clients must retain new lawyers to go to court. Thus, the collaborative lawyers are completely focused on helping the parties reach agreement; they are not distracted by the need to gird themselves for battle. No lawyers "stirring the pot" or "churning the case."

Why are you so excited about Collaborative Law?

Because it's a positive change, a change for the better! Today, when someone files for divorce, it's always a race to the courthouse, because the first to file has the advantage. And it is war from the get-go; that petition for divorce is always a shot across the bow. It's *destructive*, not only financially, but also emotionally.

And, if there are children, they are *always* caught in the middle. Even when my client "wins," it never *feels* like we won.

Unlike traditional divorce, the Open Palm Divorce is *constructive.* First, neither party has the advantage; they are always on equal footing. And, instead of being adversaries, the lawyers serve as teachers and problem-solvers in a quest to create the best possible resolution for both parties. The parties learn to problem solve, to identify what they *need* instead of just talking about what they *want.*

What do you mean? How does that work?

We work to identify the parties' underlying concerns, rather than what they say they want, so . . . "I want the house" really means "I want security," "I want the best schools for my kids," "I want to be close to my neighbors." "I want the kids 90% of the time" means "I don't want to pay you child support." "I want 50% of everything," means, "I want my fair share."

How does this differ from mediation?

Mediation is an event; the purpose of mediation is to get the parties to compromise enough to end their marriage. And mediation is a free look at the other side's case, in case you end up in trial. Mediation is confidential, but, if you go to trial anyway, you can still use the information you discovered during mediation.

Collaborative law is a process; the parties learn how to problem solve and how to move forward. If they have children, they learn to work together in their continuing and different relationship as co-parents.

Why?

Because it's not over, even when it's over; for example, you are always parents together, like it or not. You choose *Open Palm*, in part, because it's not just about the divorce!

Why are you so gung-ho about this?

We are told that "50% of first marriages . . . 67% of second marriages . . . and 74% of third marriages end in divorce." Divorce is rampant. Like a stone thrown into a pond, court divorce has an adverse impact on everyone, because it ripples outward. Not only on the parties, but on their children, the grandparents, their neighbors, their employers . . . . Everyone! I made this point to a banker I met recently, and he replied that his neighbor had subpoenaed him to testify just the week before!

And no one learns anything in the process. Not only do people get divorced again and again, but, even after their divorce is over, they go back to court again and again!

On the other hand, the Open Palm Divorce will teach folks how to problem solve, how to work with each other to resolve their disputes. And it will equip them with techniques to work through problems they may have in their future relationships. It even sometimes helps them to solve the problems in their current relationship; I've heard of parties reconciling during the process!

Collaborative law is at the tipping point. And the ripple effect that collaborative law will have on our society can only be positive.

What are the pluses to Collaborative Law, aside from teaching people how to problem solve?

1. It's confidential.
   The parties' financial information;
   The parties' family issues (dirty laundry like addictions, domestic violence, affairs, and mental health issues);
   Look at the celebrities who have used collaborative divorce (Robin Williams, T'Boone Pickens, Madonna, Tiger Woods, Guy Ritchie, and Cameron Crowe).
   Is it the same as "sealing" the court file?
   No, generally, "sealing" just means that everything is placed in a manila envelope marked "sealed." Any with access to the file can still open the envelope. In collaborative law, the documents are never placed in the court file in the first place.
2. It's less expensive.
3. The spouses make the decisions, not some judge who doesn't know them or their children, or share their values.
4. It protects relationships instead of fostering wars between people who used to care about each other.

How much does a court divorce cost?

Let me put it this way: it can cost as much as you want, but it can't cost as little as you want; it's not just in one party's control! I have seen everyday divorces that cost as much as $50-100,000 per spouse. I have seen people with millions of dollars spend over a million dollars each on their attorneys and expert witnesses.

What does the cost depend on?

A number of factors:

- Children
- House
- Alimony
- Business valuation
- Investments
- Retirement accounts
- Number of experts
- Age of the children
- Wealth and resources of the parties
- Pets (yes, I once represented a husband in a divorce where the only question was who would get the dogs . . .)
- But most importantly, the animosity between the parties!

What about the Open Palm Divorce?

Well, you know intuitively that it'll be less, just by its very nature.

Why?

No Perry Mason stuff! No discovery; no motions; no trial; no battle of the experts . . .
Plus, every team member does what he does best

- The financial neutral works on the finances;
- The facilitator works on the emotional issues;
- The lawyers coach their clients on the legal issues and the problem solving]

And it's less stressful. Any divorce is difficult. The Open Palm Divorce is just easier. We call it the kinder, gentler divorce. People think of divorce as a legal process with an emotional component. In truth, it's an emotional process with a legal component. We ignore this truth in the court divorce; in the collaborative divorce, we recognize it by relying on the "coach" or "facilitator."

Who is the coach?

A mental health professional, who defuses the emotional bombs that would explode during litigation.

What do the judges think of collaborative divorce?

Well, they love it, of course. They are supportive not only because they have more than enough work to do as it is, but because they know that their rulings are based on limited information. How can you reduce a 15-year marriage with three children to a one-, maybe a two-day trial? People should make decisions based on their intimate knowledge of their families, rather than relying on a third party who, as a judge once explained to me, only sees a snapshot of their lives before deciding issues they will have to live with for the rest of their lives.

Is Collaborative Law limited to divorces?

Absolutely not. It is applicable to any dispute. It would obviously work in a partnership or corporate dispute, which is, after all, a business divorce. But we've also trained probate lawyers and employment attorneys in collaborative dispute resolution, as well. I can see the collaborative law process operating in any area where the parties disagree.

I understand that the collaborative process is a constructive approach to dissolution of marriage? Why do you say that?

Courtroom divorce is very destructive. Everyone knows that. It's war from the get-go. Collaborative divorce, conversely, is constructive, teaching the clients skills such as . . .

You say that your clients learn problem solving, communication, parenting, and partnering skills. How do you do that?

Part of the collaborative process involves individual client meetings with the facilitator. The facilitator is expert in these skills. The facilitator discusses these skills directly with the clients and sometimes even gives them homework to help them hone those skills. But the process also involves team meetings. At these, the lawyers model these skills for their clients. The clients learn from the modeling that goes on in front of them, working through with the team, but also with each other, the very issues raised in their dissolution of marriage.

What was your most touching experience in a collaborative divorce?

There actually have been three. I call them:

1. *The Apology*
2. *The Secret*
3. *The Lesson*

Discuss details

What was the worst courtroom divorce you've been involved in?

The Grandfather Divorce – discuss details

How has practicing collaborative divorce changed your life?

Judges say that they see the worst of good people in divorce court and the best of bad people in criminal court. I get to see the best side of good people in collaborative divorce.

Thank you so much for being here. If people would like a copy of your book, they can visit Amazon.com or I-books. Or for more information, e-mail Joryn@OpenPalmLaw.com.

Appendix 6
Sample Story Blog

The Secret

Tampa's Bay Area Legal Services recently referred Tabitha Jamison to me for help with her divorce. Tabitha is a matronly woman of color, with striking clear green eyes, whose face is usually crinkled in a radiant smile. She is habitually dressed in a professional-looking pants suit. Because she only makes $8,800 a year and lives in a leased apartment, she qualifies for *pro bono* services.

After I explained her options — the kitchen table divorce, the mediated divorce, and the traditional courtroom brawl, among others — she opted for the collaborative choice. She explained that she and Mr. Jamison had separated over 12 years earlier. Although he had had two more children by two different women since, and had one from before they married, *and* she believed that his current girlfriend might be pregnant, they had continued while separated to co-parent their own two children amicably. She saw no reason why their divorce should change that.

Chuck Jamison made approximately $60,000 a year, he had five children by four different women, and his current girlfriend was pregnant. All of his children lived with their mothers, but he spent substantial amounts of time with each. He religiously maintained *all* of his child support payments.

The standards of our *pro bono* project permit me to make the judgment call, so I found him a lawyer who was willing to take his part on a *pro bono* basis, as well. Chuck agreed to participate with Tabitha on a collaborative approach to their divorce. His lawyer, Eric, and I chose the facilitator, Melinda, and the neutral financial professional, Tanya, and both of them agreed to volunteer their time.

The clients each met with both Melinda and Tanya. The professional team and our shadows (professionals trained collaboratively but who had not yet handled a collaborative divorce themselves) held a conference call thereafter to discuss the case details as we each understood them. Thus, the facilitator shared with us her perspective on the wife's anger, caused by her perception of her husband's recent selfishness. Over the last few years, he'd been less forthcoming when she asked for extra money towards the children's expenses.

Her irritation came to a head because their daughter was turning sixteen and wanted a special *Sweet Sixteen* party. Tabitha's research showed that it would cost $2500 for the party that her daughter wanted, and that was more than she alone could pay. Her anger rose when she approached Chuck to discuss it. He simply said that he couldn't afford to help her and failed to even offer to contribute. Until recently he had never been so close-mouthed; they used to be able to talk about everything. She didn't know what had changed, but she was fed up!

During our first full team meeting, we reviewed the particulars of the collaborative participation agreement and ensured that everyone present — the shadows, as well as the entire working team — had executed it. We identified the clients' interests, which were not complicated. There was no personal property to distribute, no home to argue over, and their long separation left neither asking for alimony.

Nevertheless, we proceeded judiciously. Our team had never worked together before, and we were cautious; we didn't know what the team dynamic would be yet and we wanted to ensure that we were communicating and collaborating well together.

Tabitha began, explaining that her number one interest was in providing higher education for their two children. No one in either her family or in Chuck's had attended college, including his oldest son, now nineteen, by his first wife. She appreciated that Chuck had already had lengthy discussions with their two children about the advantages of higher education. Tabitha emphasized her regret and frustration that she had never been able to go. She beamed when she told us how well her fifteen-year-old girl and fourteen-year-old boy had done in school. Despite the daughter's near-blindness, she believed they both would continue to excel beyond high school.

Tabitha did not mention, at this point, that she wanted Chuck to increase her child support. Because his earlier-born child, a nineteen-year-old, was no longer in school or legally entitled to his support, she believed this was fair. She did emphasize that Chuck was a wonderful father, always available for parent-teacher conferences, always available to be the disciplinarian when she needed his support, always there for their kids, and always understanding of both their children and of her.

This led to her concern over Chuck's inexplicable selfishness, particularly regarding the *Sweet Sixteen* party. Melinda ensured that Tabitha was able to fully express her feelings about this issue and that she had no other interests that she wanted to cover. Only then did she ask Chuck to express his interests.

Chuck was the same age as Tabitha, but he looked older. He was a handsome man, and also dressed in business casual—a nice pair of trousers and a golf shirt, with a closely cropped haircut and a clean-shaven face. He did not smile when he explained what a wonderful mother Tabitha was now, had always been, and how much he valued that in her. He completely affirmed her desire for their kids to go to college and earn bachelor's degrees. That would make him very happy.

However, he emphasized, his primary concern was to ensure that his children were *citizens* of the United States. They were growing up in the best country on earth, at the best time possible, and he wanted so very much for them to *be* citizens. That meant that they would make a contribution, that they would understand that *they* were important, and that *they* could make a difference.

His passionate comments generated a long pause around the table. At this point his attorney asked if Chuck would feel comfortable sharing what they had discussed in their off-line meeting earlier in the week. Chuck hesitated for a long moment before he said, "Yes." He then turned in his chair slightly, but noticeably (to me, at least) away from Tabitha and myself and towards Eric and Melinda, the facilitator.

He looked down at the surface of the table for another lengthy silence, and then began, "I never thought I'd have to say this." He paused. "But I know what it's like to be *America's Most Wanted*." He continued to face Eric and Melinda; he avoided addressing Tabitha. "I had a great job with the railroad. But a few years ago, I was laid off. So, I applied for unemployment."

Tabitha nodded; she remembered.

"My unemployment insurance helped me pay the bills, but it couldn't cover all of my child support, as well." He paused again. "I hoped the railroad would rehire me, or find me another job, so I continued to look for other positions with the railroad. But it was a long time, and I exhausted my savings just keeping my child support payments current.

"Eventually, I found a part-time job. It was minimum wage but I thought it was better than nothing. The money I made from that job, and other part-time jobs I was able to find, together with my unemployment, allowed me to pay my child support without missing a beat."

Chuck took a deep breath, and continued with his story. Eventually, the railroad rehired him for his old job and his life returned to normal. Throughout this time, none of his children ever lacked for his child support. Then he got the phone call. At first, he didn't grasp its significance; a woman called from the railroad board and asked to meet with him. He set a time outside of business. But then his plans went awry, so he called to postpone and reschedule.

When she replied, "Let's just meet at the police station," he realized that this was more serious than he had understood.

The following series of events blurred together for him. As requested, he went to the police station, where he met with the woman and a federal investigator. They accused him of defrauding the federal government. Unbeknownst to him, his minimum-wage part-time jobs had violated the railroad's unemployment conditions. He had been under the mistaken impression that any part-time position was acceptable as long as it wasn't for a railroad. The federal investigator threatened him with ten years in prison if he didn't plead guilty to fraud for each two-week period that he had reapplied for unemployment while earning money part-time.

Of course, he retained a lawyer, but his limited resources forced him to borrow against his retirement funds in order to pay for legal fees. His attorney recommended that he accept the plea bargain; plead guilty to all 25 counts of fraud in exchange for five years of probation and complete restitution. He agreed to pay back all of the unemployment money he had received while he worked part time. With his back against the wall, he had no choice but to sign on the dotted line.

At this point, Chuck's eyes were moist. Although *he* wasn't crying, it took all of my self-control to contain my own tears. And I was not the only one at the table who was affected.

Then Chuck detailed his fears about being on house arrest while awaiting his sentencing. Would his children know something was wrong when they visited? How could he hide it from them? Would they notice that he wouldn't step outside the front door during their sleepovers? Thankfully, they did not.

At his sentencing hearing, the man preceding him pled guilty to selling two hundred and fifty pounds of cocaine. The man following admitted to setting up a pyramid scheme, defrauding old folks of their retirement funds. When Chuck faced the judge to discuss his plea bargain, he was unable to agree that he was guilty of the crimes with which he'd been charged. The judge was adamant that he should show some remorse. However, Chuck stood his ground. He had not intended to commit fraud; he had simply been ignorant. As a former prosecutor, I realized how lucky Chuck had been. After the judge castigated him far more severely than either the preceding man or the one following him, he approved the negotiated plea bargain.

Chuck will remain on probation until 2018. He is paying the restitution, as well as repaying the retirement fund loan he withdrew to pay his lawyer. With no money to spare, he has no resources to help with the *Sweet Sixteen* celebration. He'd been unable to tell Tabitha why, until now—with the help of our facilitator and the rest of the collaborative team.

At this point, an hour and forty minutes into our first full team meeting, I suggested a break.

Tabitha and I met off-line; I wanted her reaction to Chuck's news outside of the team environment because her body language had signaled extreme anger to me. She was fairly vibrating with fury as she explained that she and Chuck had been friends since high school, and had always been able to talk to each other. She was furious that he had not trusted her enough to confide in her.

When I asked her to trust me; she agreed. I explained that I understood her feelings of betrayal, but asked her to consider his view, to try to stand in his shoes for just a moment.

"Tabitha, I think that preserving your respect for him, and even more importantly, your children's respect for him, was so important to Chuck that he's been unwilling to risk losing it by confiding in you. Now, in this safe environment, he felt that he could tell you."

While she sat deep in thought, I waited for her reaction.

When she finally responded, I knew my words had struck a chord. She acknowledged that his feelings for her were more complex than she had imagined. She agreed to consider the new information and to reassess past events in light of it. I begged her not to confront Chuck in the meantime, but instead to meet with Melinda, our facilitator, to help her process. We went back to the meeting and asked to adjourn until the next full team meeting in a few weeks.

A few days after we adjourned, Melinda sent the following e-mail:

> I spoke with Tabitha today. She is doing fine. She said that she and Chuck actually spoke yesterday after the meeting and processed what happened a little more. Then they went on to discuss Kasey's *Sweet Sixteen*. She said they are in a good place. She thought the meeting went really well.

Here's the thing: the outcome would have been far different with traditional trial attorneys and other litigation-oriented professionals. One result could have included either Tabitha's lawyer uncovering the fact that he is now a felon, or Chuck spilling his guts in the courtroom. Either way, he would have been humiliated by Tabitha's attorney, and undoubtedly his kids would eventually have learned of his embarrassing conviction.

The other possibility is that his conviction would have remained secret, and Tabitha would have continued to believe that he'd simply become a selfish son of a bitch. Either way, their efforts to co-parent effectively would have been tragically compromised, and their children would have lost the benefit of having two congenial parents working in unity together.

Let there be no doubt that proceeding collaboratively was the best option that this couple could have elected. We were now well on our way to helping Tabitha and Chuck finalize the dissolution of their marriage while remaining amicable parents of the children they share, and who still respect them both.

Appendix 7
Sample Top Ten Tips Blog

Surprising Relationship Tips
Divorce Lawyers Could Share If They Wanted To

Understand that marriage is hard work. Commence your marriage with the idea that you will both work together on "being married" every day. Being married is not a state of being; it is a work in progress. And it *is* work. So, don't ignore problems when you first notice them. Work on them before they blow up and explode. Treat your spouse like a date every day. Notice the little things that attracted you to begin with and enjoy them every day; don't take them for granted. Don't allow familiarity to breed contempt.

Understand that your spouse-to-be will not change. My divorcing clients share why they are getting divorced; they often knew about their spouse's behavior "flaw" or their relationship disconnect prior to getting married. About 95% of the time, they believed that it would change. Your spouse will not change, and, in fact, those little imperfections will only worsen over time. Realize early what they are, and determine if you can live with them forever before you tie the knot.

Consider whether to sign a prenuptial agreement. It gives you a way out and marriage is a forever commitment. Do you really want that? If you're not ready to promise that you will stay together through thick or thin, perhaps you should not get married. While most attorneys will advise that a prenuptial agreement is a wise financial move, a wiser move is to wait to marry someone to whom you can really make that permanent pledge.

Marry someone who shares your financial views. Money is the most common cause of divorce; folks have diverse philosophies about how to handle the finances and, once they are teamed together in marriage, never really address how to harmonize their different value systems. They start out in love, and small disconnects go unnoticed. Later, when they are comfortable, they overlook larger disconnects; later still, they discount them. At some point, their differences become too great to ignore; they can't make excuses anymore. Because the couple has never learned to address them, the financial issues have caused rifts in their abilities to communicate, to problem solve, and to grow together.

Decide to grow together. Let's talk about the finances again. Many people marry before they have solidified their views on many issues, spending included. So, take classes on spending, on child rearing, on religion, and on other sensitive topics before the issues start raising their ugly heads. Get educated together. This will ensure that you both have the same information. Then decide together how you will handle complex issues, before they arise and become emotional.

GO TO A MARRIAGE COUNSELOR (OF SOME KIND) EARLY AND OFTEN. Seeing a counselor should not be an admission of failure; it should be like signing up for guitar lessons or for Tae Kwon Do. If you can't think of a good reason to go, I can: go to work on your communication, problem-solving, or co-parenting skills.

ENSURE THAT YOU BOTH HAVE THE SAME DAY OFF ONCE A WEEK. Maintaining a strong relationship takes time together. Stay in bed together one morning a week and talk, in bed. No agenda. Well, if there's any agenda, it's just to cuddle. If you have to brush your teeth first, get up and do that and then get back in bed. Lock the door; no kids. Cuddle. (One of you needs that, and the other one will find that s/he enjoys it more than s/he thinks s/he will.)

SHARE A HOBBY. Again, it is important to spend time together. You don't have to share all of the same hobbies, but it is important to share most of them, considering that our hobbies consume much of what little free time we enjoy. Run races. Play golf. Watch movies. Play music together. My husband insists on running the weekend errands with me, instead of splitting up to get them done in twice the time. (I brag about this all the time, even though he first made this declaration 22 years ago!) Whatever interests you share, engage in them together. And if you don't share them, then one of you must change your interest. My husband took up golf; I had no interest. But he was spending six hours every week out on a golf course somewhere so I took it up, too. I developed an interest, if not in the sport itself, at least in the nature I enjoyed while out on the course, and, more importantly, in the talking we did while we were out there.

SHOWER OR BATHE TOGETHER EVERY DAY. My husband and I purposely installed a double-headed shower. At least twice a week, we shower at the same time. It's a great time to plan, and especially to discuss matters outside of the hearing of little ears. My associate's parents bathed together every night, and she and her husband now follow that same practice. It is a great time to unwind. Either way, it's easy to add to busy schedules because you both need to bathe, so you're not adding anything additional to your schedules. And it's good to be naked with each other every day. It is something private and special that you only share with another, so it will keep you connected. And you never know where it will lead! Which segues into my next tip . . . .

NEVER STOP HAVING SEX. It is the one thing that you share together that you do not share with anyone else. Even if you are best friends, you are more than that . . . you are spouses whose relationship initially grew because of your sexual intimacy with one another. Sex is a basic, biological need. As a married couple, you depend on one another to meet this need. Even if you are tired, not in the mood, or not even attracted to your spouse in that moment, make sex a regular part of your relationship. Vow to make love at least once a week. If you get to the end of a week without having done so, do whatever it takes to be intimate before the clock strikes midnight on the seventh day. It will also add an element of fun to your relationship!

Know that the grass isn't greener. While it may be tempting to explore a new, exciting, attractive, and interesting person, remember that that person comes with his or her own set of flaws. The turmoil that an affair brings with it is not worth the excitement, and people do not end up any happier once the dust settles. Be happy with the one you have, and actively work together to remember why you chose each other.

Don't give up too soon. Remember that you vowed to be together "for better, for worse," and sometimes, it's a "for worse" period. But, this too shall pass. The good times will return if you weather the storm together and don't jump ship.

Appendix 8
Reading List

From Lawyer to Law Firm, How to Manage a Successful Law Business
Liz Miller & Joryn Jenkins

Become a Key Person of Influence
Daniel Priestly

Becoming a Person of Influence
John Maxwell

Developing the Leader Within You
John C Maxwell

How to Win Friends & Influence People
Dale Carnegie

Switch
Chip Heath & Dan Heath

Dig Your Well Before You're Thirsty
Harvey Mackay

Givers Gain: The BNI Story
Misner & Morris

The World's Best-Known Marketing Secret
Ivan Misner

Room Full of Referrals
Alessandra, Misner, & Lyons

Leadership and Self-Deception
The Arbinger Institute

The Greatest Salesman in the World
Og Mandino

How I Raised Myself from Failure to Success in Selling
Frank Bettger

On Speaking Well
Peggy Noonan

Creating Wealth
Robert Allen

The New Positioning
Jack Trout

Killing Sacred Cows
Garrett Gunderson

Boom, Seven Choices for Blowing the Doors Off Business as Usual
Kevin & Jackie Freiburg

The Art of Mingling
Jeanne Martinet

Ruthless Focus
Thomas Hall

See You at the Top
Zig Ziglar

Silos, Politics, and Turf Wars
Patrick Lencioni

The Story Factor
Annette Simmons

Improving Your Story Telling
Doug Lipman

The No Asshole Rule
Robert I. Sutton

The Checklist Manifesto
Atul Gawande

The 4-Hour Workweek
Timothy Ferriss

Blink
Malcolm Gladwell

The Tipping Point
Malcolm Gladwell

Outliers
Malcolm Gladwell

Get a Grip
Wickman and Paton

Traction
Gino Wickman

Rocket Fuel
Wickman and Mark C. Winters

Talk Like Ted
Carmine Gallo

Thank You for Arguing
Jay Heinrichs

Never Eat Alone
Keith Ferrazzi

Good to Great
Jim Collins

The Dream Manager
Matthew Kelly

Guts
Kevin and Jackie Freiberg

Words That Work, It's Not What You Say, It's What People Hear
Dr. Frank Luntz

Think Big, Act Small
Jason Jennings

Unthink
Eric Whal

Dare
Gary Leboff

Art of War
Sun Tsu

Influence, the Psychology of Persuasion
Robert B Cialdini, PhD

The Seven Habits of Highly Effective People
Stephen R. Covey

The Eighth Habit, From Effectiveness to Greatness
Stephen R. Covey

First Things First
Covey, Merrill, and Merrill

The Speed of Trust
Stephen M. R. Covey

The Tao of Negotiation
Edelman and Crain

StrengthsFinder
Tom Rath

How to Win a Pitch
Joey Asher

Conscious Capitalism
Mackey & Sisodia

Trust Me, I'm Lying
Ryan Holiday

No Fear Speaking
Joe Yazbeck

The Art of Social Media
Kawasaki & Fitzpatrick

Appendix 9
Sample Foreword Request

Dear Celebrity So-and-So,

I hope this letter finds you well. As you may be aware, I am passionate about the collaborative divorce movement. As such, I have heard wonderful things about what you have done to advance knowledge of this concept in the public consciousness.

In an effort to add strength to the collaborative process movement and to support its practitioners, I have written two books. The first is titled *War or Peace (Avoid the Destruction of Divorce Court)* and was published this past September. I enclose a copy for your scrutiny. Stu Webb was gracious enough to write the foreword to that volume, and, as you can see, both Pauline Tesler and Norma Trusch wrote testimonials in its support.

In *War or Peace*, I discuss the various choices for couples who are embarking on the path to divorce and why the collaborative process option is often their best alternative. Then I proceed to offer a roadmap to the process.

My second book, *I Never Saw My Father Again (The Divorce Court Effect)*, extends the discussion initiated in *War or Peace* by elaborating more on the collaborative team members and their functions, as well as on how to make the process more effective. This second book debuts in May.

I have a huge favor to ask. Would you consider writing the foreword to this second book? I know how busy you must be; I would be happy to prepare a draft for you to work from.

Thank you so much for your consideration. I will call on *** to follow up on my request.

Yours Very Truly,

APPENDIX 10
SAMPLE TESTIMONIAL REQUESTS

CLIENT

The reason I'm calling today is because I value and respect your opinion. As a former client of mine, I want to give you sneak peek into a new service I'm offering and the book I'm writing about it. I need some outside viewpoints and because I value your opinion, I can't think of anyone I'd rather have review the book and tell me what you think. I've included a PDF of the book here, and, if you could read at least a couple of chapters that would be great.

Would you be willing to help me out? I'm on a deadline. When can I expect to hear back from you?

COLLEAGUE

I e-mail you today because I value your opinion as an expert in the field of ***. As you know, I've been writing a new book on the subject.

It would mean the world to me if I could cite you as one of the experts in the book and get your opinion as to whether it has merit and value. I apologize in advance for the imposition, but if you are able to take a few minutes out of your day to look through and review it, I would be very grateful. I am hoping to publish within the next four weeks. I have therefore attached a PDF of the book to this e-mail. If you are able to give me some feedback by this time next week, I would be happy to draft the testimonial for you from that. You could then put your own personal spin on it.

Please let me know if this plan meets with your approval. And thank you so very much considering my request.

CELEBRITY

I have a current book in production. The information inside is relevant and meaningful to ***. While I understand that *** is a very busy person, it would mean the world to me if I could get her stamp of approval, her personal spin on my book. The book is going to be published through *Open Palm Press* next month. I would very much like to feature *** as one of the testimonials. I've included a PDF of the book here. Will you would be so kind as to pass this information on to her and get her opinion?

If all of this is acceptable to ***, I would be happy to save her time by preparing three-to-four separate sound bites. She could then personalize the one that best suits her.

*   *   *

This last request netted me a testimonial from Laura Wasser, "Divorce Lawyer to the Stars" and author of *It Doesn't Have to Be That Way: How to Divorce Without Destroying Your Family or Bankrupting Yourself*, as well as one from Hon. Andrew P. Napolitano, Senior

Judicial Analyst, Fox News Channel; former judge of the Superior Court of New Jersey, among others.

Appendix 11
Sample Audience Feedback Form

It can be challenging for professionals to obtain information in advance that will help them choose the best training and trainer to meet their unique needs. There are significant differences in how trainers approach their material and in their individual qualities as trainers and motivators of excellence. For these reasons, personal comments from attendees can be immensely helpful to both the trainer and the training team who chose her from among the many now being offered to the legal community.

I invite you to comment below about your reactions to this workshop, *Marketing Your Law Practice*, held in Tampa, Florida on August 26, 2016. Particularly if you found the session stimulating, valuable, challenging, and would allow me to quote you as to any unique differentiating qualities you found in me or in this program, as compared to others you've attended, I would appreciate it. By submitting this form, I appreciate your authorization for me to use your comments on my website, www.OpenPalmLaw.com, or in training event announcements and for similar purposes

I have enjoyed my time with you and your colleagues and look forward to working with you in the years to come. Thank you.

Joryn Jenkins

Your "quotable comments" about the workshop you just attended:

Your name:
Profession (Lawyer, Therapist, Financial, Business, other):
Office Location:
E-mail address:
Website:

Please e-mail a photo headshot to Joryn@OpenPalmLaw.com

Please complete the following questionnaire by circling your response to each item.

1-strongly disagree; 2-disagree; 3-neither agree nor disagree; 4-agree; 5-strongly agree

Material					
I was well informed about the workshop's objectives.	1	2	3	4	5
This seminar lived up to my expectations.	1	2	3	4	5
The content is relevant to my business.	1	2	3	4	5
I will be able to use what I learned in this seminar.	1	2	3	4	5
The difficulty level of this workshop was appropriate.	1	2	3	4	5
I would recommend this seminar to others.	1	2	3	4	5
I enjoyed this seminar.	1	2	3	4	5
Presenter					
The trainer was knowledgeable.	1	2	3	4	5
The trainer was well prepared.	1	2	3	4	5
The trainer answered my questions to my satisfaction.	1	2	3	4	5
The trainer was interesting.	1	2	3	4	5
The trainer was passionate.	1	2	3	4	5

How would you improve this training? (Check all that apply.)

___ Provide better info before the seminar.
___ Clarify the objectives.
___ Reduce the training content covered.
___ Increase the training content covered.
___ Update the content covered.
___ Improve the instructional methods.
___ Improve the material organization.
___ Decrease the difficulty.
___ Increase the difficulty.
___ Slow down the seminar pace.
___ Speed up the seminar pace.
___ Allot more time for the seminar.
___ Shorten the time for the seminar.
___ Add more video to the seminar.

APPENDIX 12
SAMPLE INFOMERCIALS

Most of my infomercials begin with "I'm a family lawyer. I help folks divorce each other without destroying their families or their savings." If it doesn't begin that way, it's still there somewhere, as in the first one below. Every one of them ends with "We're changing the way the world gets divorced!"

- Divorce is one of the most stressful events in a person's life. Divorce interferes with a person's ability to perform his job. I'm Joryn Jenkins, and I'm a family lawyer at *Open Palm Law*. I help folks divorce each other without destroying their families or their savings. Or interfering with their work. A good referral for me is a small business with 10-30 employees. Introduce me to the owner so I can tell him why collaborative divorce is good for his employees and therefore good for him!

- My best referral sources are marriage counselors, psychologists, family therapists, and life coaches. They try to keep the marriage together, but protect the family relationships when it is clear that it must end. Introduce me to any you know. They'll be glad you did.

- Why collaborative divorce?
  1 – It's confidential: the financial information; the personal information.
  2 – It's less expensive. Court divorce can cost as much as you want, but it can't cost as little as you want; it's not just in one party's control! And no Perry Mason stuff in collaborative divorce! No discovery, no motions, no battle of the experts, no trial.
  3 – It's less stressful. Courtroom divorce is difficult. But collaborative divorce is easier.
  4 – It belongs to the parties, not some judge. Clients can agree to do what judges cannot order them to do.

- My best referral sources are first responders like financial advisors; they are concerned that the family not dissipate its wealth through the divorce process, and want to retain both clients instead of losing one in the war. Introduce me to any you know. They'll be glad you did.

- Divorce is one of the most stressful events that can happen in someone's lifetime. And yet well over 50% of all marriages end in divorce. A good phrase to listen out for is "I'm through with marriage counseling," or "I'm done with her," or "I'm moving out." Refer that person to me and I'll explain his least stressful divorce choices.

- Divorce is one of the most stressful events that can happen in someone's lifetime. And yet well over 50% of all marriages end in divorce. When you refer a person to me, I'll explain the least stressful divorce choices to him or her. I tell my clients, "If you want to choose your fate, instead of letting some judge make the decisions, you should collaborate!"

- 50% of first marriages, 67% of second marriages, and 74% of third marriages end in divorce. No one learns anything constructive in the traditional divorce process. All they learn is how to go to court. Even when they're done, they go back to court over and over again. Collaborative divorce teaches folks to problem solve, to communicate better, and to work together to resolve their disagreements. It arms them with skills to work through problems in their future relationships.

- It's bad when people stay in hate-filled relationships, suffering for years in an unbearable marriage. I'm a marital surgeon. I cure diseased relationships by removing the offending part. Divorce is not the problem. An unhappy marriage is the problem; collaborative divorce is the cure.

- Who is my perfect referral source? Any "first responder," anyone who is the first to know that Jane is leaving John, that Mike is cheating on Marj, or that Adam is done with Eve. "Who?"
    - Your banker!
    - Your hair stylist!
    - Your personal trainer!
    - Your marriage counselor!
    - Your pastor!
    - Your bartender!
    - Your nail tech!

  Introduce me!

- You go to a movie; buy an overpriced ticket; pay a fortune for popcorn; watch endless coming attractions. Finally, the feature begins. It's awful. You don't want to disturb everyone, but, finally, you can't take it anymore. You sneak out, push open the exit door, and blink in the bright daylight. It's the same with marriage. You go in with high hopes; eventually you realize you've made a mistake. You don't have to be miserable until the credits roll. Divorce won't prevent you from trying again. Get a collaborative divorce.

- It's hard to leave an awful movie without disturbing anyone, sneaking down the crowded aisle in the dark. There is another way to exit a packed theater. Yell "fire!" at the top of your lungs. Then, of course, you create a stampede. People get shoved and pushed and bruised and even trampled. And it takes longer to leave than if you had carefully picked your way down the aisle. That is what traditional divorce looks like.

- The fact is, you never get your day in court . . . in court. It's called "no-fault" divorce. The judge isn't interested in whether he cheated with her best friend or she spent all their money on the slots. It's all irrelevant. But not in collaborative divorce, where you get your day in court. It's just not in court.

- Happy New Year! Now that the holidays are over, folks who have been putting off their divorces are making New Year's Resolutions, planning a fresh start in their relationships. If you have a friend like this, be a friend! Recommend that they consult with Open Palm law for a win-win divorce!

- Courtroom divorce pits parents against each other in a war with no winners. The best part about this archaic process? It's recorded in a public court file for the whole world to see, including the kids. But there is a better way . . . mediation. Use an expert with a single goal: to dissolve your marriage peacefully. Send them to Open Palm Law where we can mediate their divorce.

- Collaborative divorce takes place over a series of meetings: between the clients and the neutral financial, the facilitator, the lawyer, the whole team. No judge; no court. If the parties throw in the towel and file, their lawyers are done, and they retain new lawyers. Collaborative lawyers are focused on finding peaceful resolution. They are not distracted by the need to gird themselves for battle. No lawyers "stirring the pot" or "churning the case.

- This is an open palm. This is a closed fist. An open palm holds more than a closed fist. This is collaborative divorce. [Open palm.] This is traditional divorce. [Fist.] A collaborative divorce holds families together (even though the parents may not be). [Palms cupped together.] A traditional courtroom divorce blows families apart. [Fist explodes open.] Send your friends to a collaborative lawyer for their divorces.

- The divorce rate more than doubled between 1940 and 1981 before falling a third, to a 40-year low, by 2009. What caused this plunge? The recession! 1) we couldn't afford to get divorced *and* 2) we had nothing to fight over! Now, divorces are on the rise! Retain Open Palm Law and keep more of what's yours!

- Don't assume a divorce lawyer is too expensive; it's not the rate or the retainer that determine the cost. It's the hours! An Open Palm Law divorce will take less court and less time.

- For years, I had a horrible job. I was a great trial attorney. But trial attorneys have been doing it all wrong. Going to court to dissolve marriages. Taking your most personal issues in front of a judge who doesn't know you . . . Doesn't share your values . . . Doesn't love your children . . . Now I tell my clients, "Don't litigate; collaborate!"

- Collaborative divorce is cutting edge. It's divorce with diplomacy and with dignity, divorce without court. It's a win-win, peaceful process that gets you divorced but protects your relationships with your children, your extended family, your friends, and everyone else you know!

- Why collaborative divorce instead of the traditional courtroom divorce? When you file for divorce, it's always a race to the courthouse; the first to file has the advantage. It's war from the get-go. It's destructive, financially *and* emotionally, for the clients and their kids. Even when we "win," it never feels like we won. Collaborative divorce is constructive. Neither party has the advantage; they are always on equal footing. The lawyers serve as teachers and problem-solvers, not adversaries, finding the best possible resolution for both parties. The parties learn to problem solve, to identify what they need instead of what they want.

- Remember the 50/50 rule: 50% of first marriages end in divorce and, usually, 50% of the assets go to each spouse! When divorce is inevitable, don't litigate; mediate!

- I was talking to the founder of *Evos* the other day explaining collaborative divorce to him. I said, "We are doing for 'divorce' what you did for 'fast food.' We offer "the healthy alternative.'" His response? "That's so weird; it just makes the hair on my arms stand up!' That's a great service you're providing!" A great referral for me is your pastor, your minister, your rabbi, someone who counsels folks about their most personal problems.

- Collaborative divorce is a divorce process in which a couple can end their marriage without starting World War III. But if you walk into my office wanting to start World War III with your spouse, we can do that, too. War or peace? It's your choice.

- The dream divorce. A divorce where the spouses do not hate each other at the end. A divorce where the spouses can actually agree on how to separate their lives from each other while still parenting their children together, where, afterwards, they can be friendly with each other instead of bitter and hate-filled. This is the type of divorce my firm provides, collaborative divorce.

APPENDIX 13
SAMPLE BRIEF POWERPOINT (BROCHURE)

This is a 14-slide brochure. While the rule of thumb is generally that a speaker can cover one slide every three minutes, I tend to speak more rapidly and cover more information, especially when the presentation is limited to a very specific topic, like this one. I can easily cover this presentation in half an hour.

How to Create a Company Brochure

www.OpenPalmLaw.com

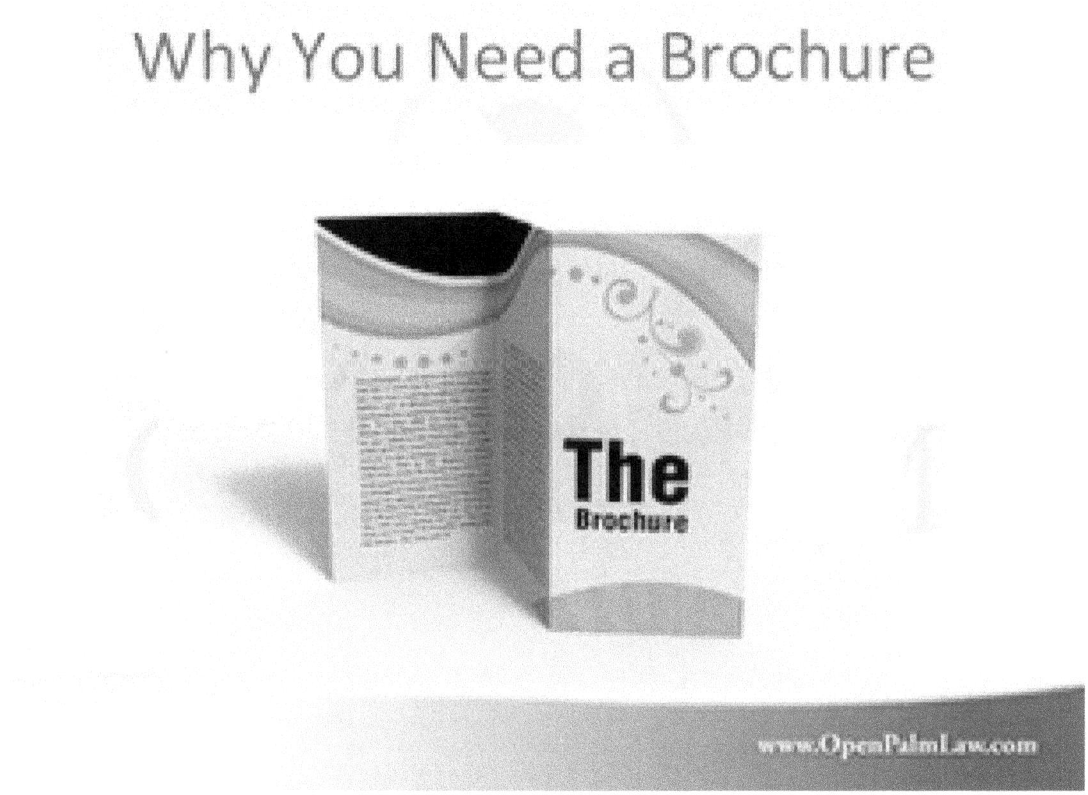

- A company brochure showcases your mission and vision.
- It includes more information than your business card, so potential clients and colleagues can get a true taste of who you are and what you are about.
- It clearly and succinctly outlines what a company is about and what it has to offer.
- It highlights your services for customers and why they should choose you over the competition.
- It is a good way to advertise your business.

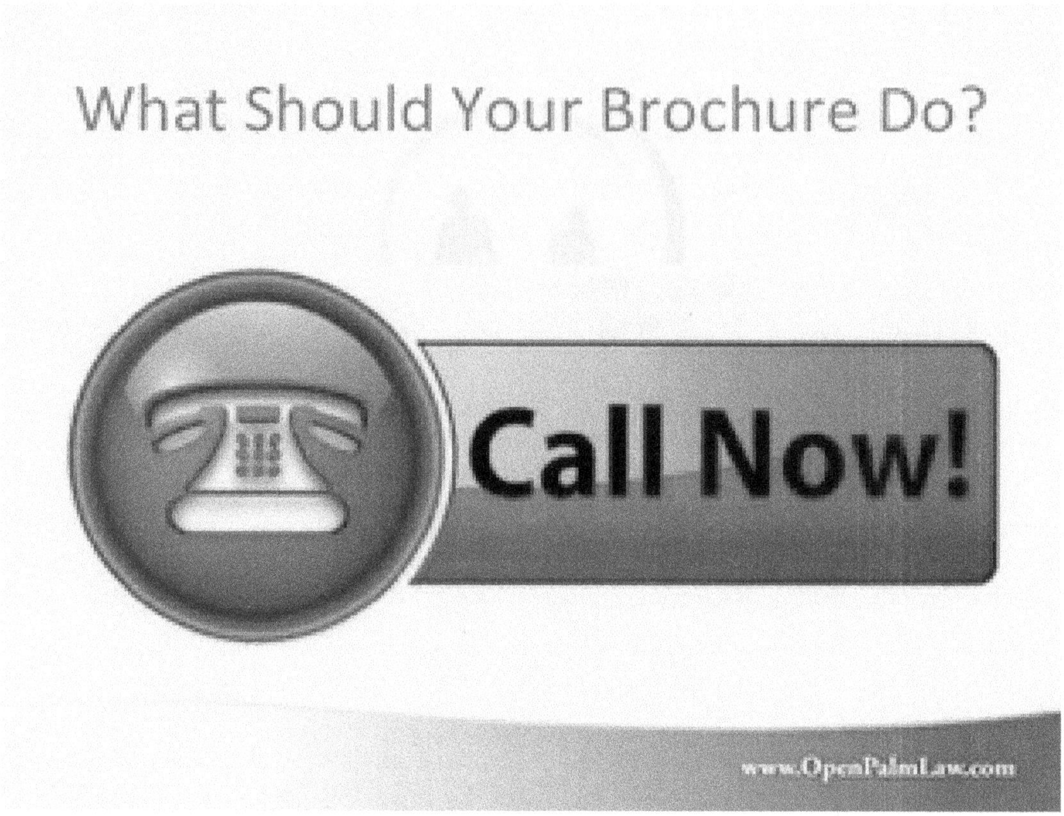

- Your brochure should grab your reader's attention, get him interested enough to read further, raise his desire for your service, and provoke him to call and make an appointment.
- Focus on the benefits the reader will enjoy by retaining you.

- Before preparing your brochure, create an avatar of your perfect client. In family law practice, your avatar will likely be people going through a family law dispute who have minor children, assets and liabilities, and enough funds to afford to get a divorce. Also, your avatar will be other family law, financial, and mental health professionals with whom you would like to work, or first responders who can send you clients.
- Once you have constructed your avatar, determine the burning question that they would like answered in your brochure. Talk to former clients and colleagues to get an idea of what you should include. Why would they want to buy your services? Because you are a great trial attorney, your clients love you, or you are less expensive than other lawyers? Why?

- Microsoft Word's preloaded templates are not very helpful, but Microsoft's Office website has almost one hundred free brochure and booklet templates. You can find additional free Word brochure templates on HP's website for small and medium-size businesses.
- If you have a Mac, try Apple's iWork Pages ,which features basic templates. Additional free iWork templates can be found on the iWork Templates Blog and on iWork Community.
- You can also try PagePlus Starter Edison, MyCreativeShop, HP's Marketsplash, Epson's CreativeZone, or Brother's CreativeCenter.

Choose the thematic elements that match your business. These include a broad theme, color, and appearance of the brochure. If your business has a color scheme, design your brochure to match.

- You only have about five seconds to captures a potential reader's attention.
- Rather than featuring most prominently your company's name or logo, the most important information on your cover should be the intriguing information that will lead the reader to want to learn more.
- Be sure to use headlines and graphics on your cover that your audience cares about.
- The headline on the front of your brochure should always highlight the interests or perceived problem of your targeted audience, and be followed inside by a fuller explanation of their problems and the solutions you can provide.
- Do not include too much information on the cover.

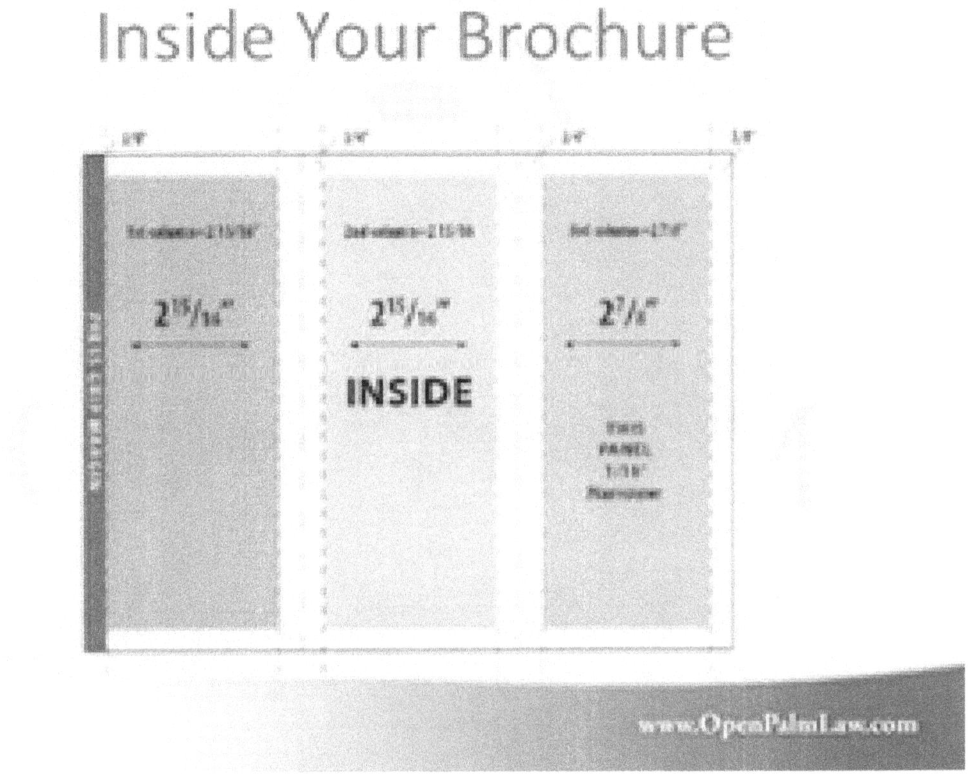

- Use benefits-oriented headlines inside your brochure.
- Use bullet points to focus on the key features of your service.
- All text should be concise and easy to read.
- Choose an easy-to-read font.
- Use 12-point font for text, 10-point font for captions, and 14 to 22-point font for headlines.
- All graphics should be attention grabbing, but not distracting or cluttered.

Put contact information, directions and/or a map on the back panel. This makes it easier for people to find your business location.

- Focus on persuasion rather than information.
- Include standard information, such as company name, at least two types of contact information, a logo, and a tagline.
- Avoid listing too much content that will overwhelm your reader. Stick to the two-to-three main points that are of interest to your target audience.
- Avoid using legal jargon and confusing words. Keep it simple. You don't want to confuse your reader.

- Always include a call to action. What do you want them to do? Call to schedule an appointment?
- Give them incentive to act now, like special discounts that are only valid before a specific date or a reminder that prices will soon be increasing.
- Ensure your business name, phone number, and website URL are easily found in the brochure.
- Establish credibility by including client testimonials.

- You may opt to print your brochures yourself. If so, make sure that you have a printer that supports two-sided (duplex) printing, or you'll spend quite a bit of time flipping over each brochure manually to print on the other side. If your printer is able to print on two sides, you'll find the option in Printer Properties menu.
- Use 16 lb. to 28 lb. paper. Use high-quality paper with a glossy finish to create a brochure that stands out.
- If you're printing over a hundred brochures, you may want to consider outsourcing the job because many print shops will include folding or assembly.

OPENPALM
WIN-WIN DIVORCE BY JORYN JENKINS
www.OpenPalmLaw.com
P 813.870.3839 • F 813.877.3839
3839 W Kennedy Blvd • Tampa, FL 33609
Joryn@OpenPalmLaw.com

Appendix 14
Speakers' Bureau Guidelines

The *Speakers' Bureau* is a core group of speakers who can knowledgeably discuss legal matters. The bureau's purpose is to provide a panel of speakers who are available to educate the public and to arrange appropriate speaking engagements for those volunteers in various venues across the community.

The mission of the bureau is to identify organizations and associations, whether community-oriented, civic, social, professional, political, religious, or cultural, that may be interested in hearing speakers present on legal issues and concerns. And then to arrange those presentations.

These guidelines will help members of the bureau's panel of speakers prepare their presentations. These guidelines will also help prospective speakers understand the objectives for the bureau in order to decide whether they wish to participate.

Guidelines

1. Speakers and prospective speakers should fully acquaint themselves with the goals and objectives of the *Speakers' Bureau*. By volunteering to participate on the speakers' panel for the bureau, a speaker agrees to provide education and training.

2. Bureau members must be bar certified attorneys.

3. Bureau members must sign a bureau membership agreement agreeing to the guidelines herein.

4. Bureau members agree to indicate that the opinions they express are solely their own and are not necessarily those of the *Speakers' Bureau*.

5. Bureau members should direct questions about the bureau and the expectations for speakers to the bureau coordinator.

6. Speakers must discuss their potential subjects with the bureau coordinator at least fourteen days prior to the presentation. The coordinator must approve the subject in writing at least ten days prior to the presentation.

7. Within seven days of a speaking engagement, the speaker must provide the bureau coordinator with a resume describing the breadth of his experience and the professional roles in which he has served, as well as the subjects on which he is prepared to speak.

8. Also within seven days of a speaking engagement, the speaker must provide the coordinator with a summary of his presentation.

9. Within three days of any presentation, the speaker must provide the coordinator with a copy of all handouts and the PowerPoint for his presentation. He must also ensure that he has prepared sufficient copies for his audience.

10. Speakers may receive reimbursement for actual expenses in making presentations. To be entitled to receive reimbursement, a speaker must provide a detailed estimate of expenses to the coordinator fourteen days prior to his presentation, as well as receipts for which he would like reimbursement within seven days after his presentation. The coordinator will provide reimbursement within seven days of receipt of the receipts. The coordinator may deny reimbursement for some or all of the speaker's expenses.

11. Speakers are responsible for determining the subjects for which they are most qualified to speak. The *Speakers' Bureau* encourages speakers to address subjects about which they have direct and detailed knowledge, broad experience, formal training, and/or personal involvement. There is no minimum experience required. A speaker's ability to address a given subject is a combination of training and quality, length, and breadth of experience.

12. Speakers should address subjects that will provide knowledge and training at all levels of experience.

13. Formal presentations (e.g., PowerPoint slides) should include a page about the *Speakers' Bureau* and how audiences may contact or otherwise connect with the *Speakers' Bureau* and its members. The coordinator will assist speakers with this information.

14. Speakers may also briefly market their own practices during presentations.

15. A speaker should direct inquiries to the bureau coordinator and/or other speakers whenever the requested subject matter is outside of his personal expertise. The coordinator will then attempt to connect the potential audience with another speaker.

16. Speakers are expected to be able to answer questions about the *Speakers' Bureau*, including its mission, values, and goals.

17. Speakers should provide the bureau coordinator with feedback after every speaking appearance.

18. Audiences will have the opportunity to provide feedback. Speakers must provide the bureau's feedback questionnaire to the audience at the end of each presentation. Speakers should be open to positive and negative feedback.

MEMBER INFORMATION – SPEAKERS' BUREAU

Personal Information

Name: ____
First *M.I.* *Last*

Business: ____
Street Address *Suite*

____
City *State* *ZIP Code*

Work Phone: ____________________ Cell Phone: ____________________

E-mail ____

Interests

I am interested in marketing: Yes No

I am interested in public speaking: Yes No

Organizations to Which You Belong

Religious: ______________________________

Charity/Service: ______________________________

Charity/Service: ______________________________

Charity/Service: ______________________________

Professional: ______________________________

Professional: ______________________________

Professional: ______________________________

Networking: ______________________________

Networking: ______________________________

Networking: ______________________________

About the Author

Joryn Jenkins is an attorney with 37 years of experience in the courtroom. She focuses her practice on courtless divorce at *Open Palm Law* in Tampa, Florida, and has made changing the way the world gets divorced® her mission. Ms. Jenkins received her B.A. from Yale University and her J.D. from Georgetown University Law Center. She is a former editor of *The Family Law Commentator* and the former editor-in-chief of both *The Federal Lawyer* and *The Bencher*, magazines with national circulations. She is the author of *The Stepmother's Cookbook* (Open Palm Press), and *Florida Civil Practice Motions* (Lexis Law Publishing). She also has authored five books on the collaborative divorce process: *War or Peace (Avoid the Destruction of Divorce Court)*; *I Never Saw My Father Again (The Divorce Court Effect)*; *A Free Divorce Handbook (How to Organize a Pro Bono Collaborative Divorce Project)*; *Open for Business (Managing Your Collaborative Practice for Passion & Profit)* and *Changing the Way the World Gets Divorced (Marketing Your Collaborative Practice)* (all Open Palm Press).

Joryn assembled the collaborative team and represented one of the spouses in the first pro bono collaborative divorce completed in Florida. She has appeared on Fox 13, ABC Action News, NBC 8, and Bay News 9, as well as on radio on *The Sam Sorbo Show, Legally Speaking, The Jamie Meloni Show, Ask the Dom,* and *Social Media Today*. She has also been featured in *The Tampa Bay Times, The Tampa Tribune,* and *The World of Collaborative Practice* e-zine, all on the subject of collaborative practice and divorce. She has also been featured in *Real Simple, Redbook,* and *Good Housekeeping* magazines, as well as published in Huffington Post.

Joryn founded the *Cheatwood American Inn of Court* in 1988, and served in its leadership until after her presidency in 2001. She co-founded the *Coordinating Council of Florida Inns* in 1989 and served on the *American Inns of Court* Board of Trustees from 1991 until 1997.

In 2001, Joryn received the *A. Sherman Christensen Award*, an award bestowed in the Supreme Court of the United States to one person once a year for her work improving ethics, professionalism, and civility in the legal profession.

The *Federal Bar Association* bestowed its highest honor, *The President's Award*, on Joryn in 1997.

JORYN'S OTHER BOOKS

Butterworth Publishers offered Joryn's first book, *Florida Civil Motions Practice*, in 1994 as part of the D&S Florida Practice Series. Lexis Law Publishing published the second edition in 1999. Recognizing that the majority of lawsuits filed in this country are won or lost in motion practice, Joryn focused on equipping her Reader to present legal and factual argument via motion effectively, efficiently, and persuasively, a prerequisite to success.

If you are interested in an introduction to the core principles raised in collaborative divorce cases, look for Joryn's first collaborative divorce book, *War or Peace (Avoid the Destruction of Divorce Court)*, on Amazon, at http://amzn.to/1C6zGG9, or on her website, at https://openpalmlaw.com/books/ or at http://bit.ly/OpenPalmBooks.

In her next book, *I Never Saw My Father Again (The Divorce Court Effect)*, Joryn explores the more complex issues of collaborative divorce in depth, and also illustrates those precepts with true stories of divorce, both collaborative and courtroom. You can find it on Amazon at http://amzn.to/1gQVzog, at https://openpalmlaw.com/books/ or at http://bit.ly/OpenPalmBooks.

In *A Free Divorce Handbook (How to Organize a Collaborative Divorce Pro Bono Project)*, Joryn explores the issues raised when a busy professional establishes a collaborative divorce *pro bono* project. Look for it on Amazon, at http://amzn.to/1YW7Rgu, or on her website, at https://openpalmlaw.com/books/ or http://bit.ly/OpenPalmBooks.

Joryn's first book in this series, *Open for Business, Managing Your Collaborative Practice for Passion & Profit* is on Amazon, at http://bit.ly/OpenForBusinessManaging. Her second, *Changing the Way the World Gets Divorced, Marketing Your Collaborative Practice*, is also on Amazon, at http://amzn.to/2nX4siV. You will also find them both on her website at https://openpalmlaw.com/books/ or at http://bit.ly/OpenPalmBooks.

Look also for Joryn's soon-to-published *From Lawyer to Law Firm, How to Build a Successful Law Business*, co-authored with Independent Law Firm Administrator Elizabeth Miller.

www.ingramcontent.com/pod-product-compliance
Lightning Source LLC
Chambersburg PA
CBHW081125180926
51611CB00004B/59
* 9 7 8 0 9 9 0 6 3 7 1 8 9 *